Contents

Planning Ahead...

WHEN TO GO

Most tourists visit Amsterdam between April and September; late March to late May is the time to see tulips in bloom. June brings the Holland Festival of art, dance, opera and theatre. Although winter can be cold and damp, December is crowded with Christmas shoppers and those staying for the festive season.

TIME

Amsterdam observes Central European Time, 1 hour ahead of GMT in winter and 2 hours in summer.

AVERAGE DAILY TEMPERATURE

JAN	FEB	MAR	APR	MAY	JUN	JUL	AUG	SEP	OCT	NOV	DEC
5°C	6°C	9°C	13°C	17°C	20°C	22°C	22°C	20°C	14°C	8°C	5°C

Spring (March to May) is at its most delightful in May – with the least rainfall.
Summer (June to August) is the sunniest of the year but good weather is never guaranteed.
Autumn (September to November) gets wetter, although September is a popular time to visit. The weather is often chilly and drizzly as winter approaches.
Winter (December to February) can be cold, and temperatures can drop so low that the canals freeze. Strong winds can increase the chill factor, and fog can blot out the sunlight for days.

WHAT'S ON

February *Carnival*: Celebrated as a preamble to Lent.
Dockers' Strike Commemmoration (29 Feb)
March *Stille Omgang* (second Sun): Silent procession.
April *National Museum Weekend* (mid-month): Museums lower entrance fees.
Koninginnedag (30 Apr): The Queens' birthday.
May *Remembrance Day* (4 May): Honours World War II victims.
Liberation Day (5 May):

Marking the end of the German Occupation in 1945.
National Windmill Day (second Sat).
National Cycling Day (second Sun).
June *Holland Festival*: International arts festival.
Grachetenloop canal race (second Sun): Along the banks of Prinsengracht and Vijzelgracht.
July *Summer Festival*: Alternative arts festival.
August *Prinsengracht-concert* (last Fri): Classical music recitals on barges outside the Hotel Pulitzer.

September *Bloemencorso* (first Sat): Flower-laden floats from Aalsmeer to Amsterdam.
National Monument Day (second Sat): Usually closed monuments and buildings open.
Jordaan Folk Festival (second week): Music, street parties.
October *Antiques Fair* (last weekend): On Spiegelkwartier.
November *Sinterklaas* (Santa Claus) *Parade* (mid-Nov).
December *Pakjesavond* (5 Dec): Traditional day for present giving.
Oudejaarsavond (31 Dec): Street parties, fireworks.

AMSTERDAM ONLINE

www.channels.nl
Use this website to take a virtual walk around the city. Pick any street and the site will display photographs and links to hotels, museums, shops or restaurants on that street. The forum is full of useful hotel and restaurant reviews written by visitors to Amsterdam.

www.amsterdam-hotels.org
www.holland-hotels.com
Accommodation: the first site represents a cross-section of hotels in the city, from budget to deluxe, including apartments and houseboats. The second covers the whole of the Netherlands, and is useful if you want to travel further afield or find hotels in nearby towns when all the hotels in Amsterdam are full. Both sites have up-to-date details of tariffs, special offers and room availability, with pictures of typical rooms and maps showing the precise location.

www.visitamsterdam.com
www.holland.com
Official tourist board sites: the first covers Amsterdam and the second the whole of the Netherlands. They are good for information about exhibitions, events and festivals. Both have an online accommodation booking, and www.visitamsterdam.com has lots of links to shops, restaurants and nightclubs. Be warned that some of the nightclub links take you to pornography sites.

www.dinnersite.
nl/_nieuw/index-e.php3
Say what kind of food you like and you'll get a comprehensive list of Amsterdam restaurants to suit.

www.bmz.amsterdam.nl/adam/index–e.html
For everything you could ever want to know about the architecture in Amsterdam, visit this excellent and informative site belonging to Amsterdam heritage.

PRIME TRAVEL SITES

www.eurostar.com
For details of international rail services.

www.ns.nl
Journey planner for getting to Amsterdam by train.

www.hollandsepot.dordt
nl/dutch/dutch.html
Fascinating information on traditional Dutch food, with recipes.

www.fodors.com
A complete travel-planning site. You can research prices and weather; book air tickets, cars and rooms; ask questions (and get answers) from fellow travellers; and find links to other sites.

CYBERCAFÉS

easyEverything,
✉ Reguliersbreestraat 22, Grachtengordel; www.easyeverything.com; open 24 hours.

Internet Café
✉ Kort Nieuwendijk 30; www.cybercafe. euronet.nl; open 10AM–midnight.

La Bastille Internet Café
✉ Lijnbaansgracht 246; www.labastille.nl; open 10AM–midnight.

5

...and Getting There

Visas are not required for EU, US or Canadian nationals, but you will need a valid passport. EU citizens can obtain health care with the production of form E111. However, insurance to cover illness and theft is strongly advised.

MONEY

The euro is the official currency of the Netherlands. Banknotes in denominations of 5, 10, 20, 50, 100, 200 and 500 euros and coins in denominations of 1, 2, 5, 10, 20 and 50 cents and 1 and 2 euros were introduced on 1 January 2002.

10 euros

50 euros

200 euros

500 euros

ARRIVING

There are direct international flights into Schiphol airport from around the world, as well as good rail connections with most European cities and regular sailings from the UK to major ferry ports, all of which have good rail connections to Amsterdam.

60 KM

Schiphol Airport ✈
Train 15 mins,
3 euros/f6.50

⛴ **Hoek van Holland ferry**
Train 1 hr 35 mins,
13.7 euros/f30.25

FROM SCHIPHOL

Schiphol (☎ 0900/0141), Amsterdam's only international airport, is 18km southwest of the city centre. Many international airlines operate scheduled and charter flights here. Trains leave the airport for Amsterdam Centraal Station every 15 minutes from 6AM until midnight, then hourly through the night. The ride takes 20 minutes and costs 3 euros/f6.50. KLM-airport buses run from the airport to a number of big hotels and you do not need to have travelled on the airline or be staying at one of the hotels to use this service. The cost is 8 euros/f17.50 one way. There are departures once or twice each hour during the day, and from 5:20–7AM and 6–10PM; you have to reserve a seat (☎ 6534975). Taxis are available but fares run as high as 31.50 euros/70f. It is usually faster to go by train to Centraal Station and take a taxi from there.

ARRIVING BY RAIL

Centraal Station has direct connections from major cities in western Europe, including high-speed links from Paris, Brussels and Cologne. From Britain, there are connections at Brussels with trains operated by Eurostar, with bargain through fares to Amsterdam. Train information: (☎ 0900/9292; www.hollandrail.com).

ARRIVING BY SEA
The major ferry ports – Ijmuiden, Rotterdam and Hoek van Holland (Hook of Holland, 80km from Amsterdam) – have good rail connections with Amsterdam. Regular sailings from the UK are offered by Stena Line, DFDS Seaways and P&O North Sea Ferries.

GETTING AROUND
Amsterdam has excellent public transport. Distances are short so you can walk or cycle to most places. But on a cold, wet day, you may be grateful to ride, and a tram trip is an attraction in its own right. The same ticket is valid for tram, bus and Metro. If you intend to use public transport frequently, buy a strip of 15 or 45 tickets (*strippenkart*) at Amsterdam's municipal transport authority, GBV and Dutch Railways ticket counters and also at the Vereniging Voor Vreemdelin-genverkeer (VVV) tourist offices (➤ 90–91).

Seventeen different tram lines have frequent service from 6AM on weekdays (slightly later on weekends) until midnight, when night buses take over, running hourly until 4AM. Day tickets are valid during the night following the day on which they were issued. If you need a ticket, board at the front and pay the driver. Take care when getting off; many stops are in the middle of the road (➤ 91).

There are four Metro lines, three terminating at Centraal Station. They are used mainly by commuters from the suburbs. The most useful city-centre station is Nieuwmarkt.

It is difficult to hail a taxi in the street. Go to a taxi stand outside major hotels, tourists attractions and Centraal Station. Ask the driver for an estimate for the journey. Water-taxis can be hailed or ordered in advance (☎ 020 6222181). Fares are high for both taxis and water-taxis.

DON'T DRIVE
Driving is not an ideal way of getting about the city because of the scarcity and high cost of public parking, the one-way streets and the large number of cyclists.

VISITORS WITH DISABILITIES
The Netherlands is one of the most progressive countries in the world when it comes to providing access and information. Hotels, museums and buildings that meet minimum standards display the International Accessibility Symbol. Tourist Information Offices have full information on hotels, restaurants, museums, tourist attractions and boat and coach excursions with facilities for people with disabilities. A special taxi service is available for people with disabilities Monday to Friday 9AM–6PM (☎ 613 4134/633 3943/655 6729); book ahead.

For further information contact the Federatie Nedelandse Gehandi-captenraad, Postbus 1693500-AD, Utrecht (☎ 30 231 3454).

Living
Amsterdam

Amsterdam Now

Above: *eating and drinking out is popular in Amsterdam*
Right: *tulips from Amsterdam – bulbs and blooms are sold throughout the city.*

A BOLD IDEA

• Radical politicians of the 1970s came up with the bold idea of providing free bicycles, painted white, that everyone could use. The idea floundered when the bikes were stolen, repainted and sold. Now the white bikes are back – but this time they can only be unlocked using an electronic smart card.

To some Amsterdam conjures the vanilla scent of waffles, barrel organs, carillons ringing out their hymns on the hour from church steeples. To others it is synonymous with tolerance – of eccentricity and of experimentation. Some people party all night and sleep off their excesses during the day; others studiously walk the canal circle, marvelling at myriad variations on the Dutch gable, or they use Amsterdam as a base for visiting the bulb fields of Haarlem, porcelain producing Delft or Edam and Gouda of cheese fame.

The city is so small that you can cross it in 30 minutes on foot; it is the capital of a country so small that it would fit into Ireland three times over. Compared with other European capitals, Amsterdam is tiny – just three quarters of a million people packed into not quite enough space. Yet for all its compact scale, it rewards frequent visits, and its constantly changing programme of

Above *Amsterdam's former stock exchange, the Beurs Van Berlage (1903), is now a concert venue*
Left: *browsing in the shop at the Van Gogh Museum*

special exhibitions, festivals, and arts events – from the wackiest avant-garde shows to the works of Rembrandt or Vermeer. The many faces of Amsterdam help make it Europe's most popular weekend-break destination.

For sheer creative energy, few cities can compete. Although the city is surrounded by light industrial estates, many who live in central Amsterdam live off their wits as academics, authors, photographers, artists, architects, journalists, lawyers and musicians. Amsterdam's university adds to the lively and youthful mix. Its various faculties (whose walls are even more plastered with graffiti than most Amsterdam

THE BELLS

● Amsterdam's carillons, high in church steeples, mark the passing of the hours all over the city by playing everything from hymns to melodies by Mozart or Beethoven. Among the best are the bells of Oude Kerk and of Westerkerk, which gave comfort to Anne Frank while she was in hiding during the 1940s.

Above: *musicians out in force on Queen's Day*
Above right: *The Bulldog coffee shop*

QUEEN'S DAY

• Nothing better sums up Amsterdam than Queen's Day, the unstuffy monarch's official birthday (30 April) and the occasion for a wild city-wide street party. Even radical Amsterdammers celebrate. Everyone wears orange, the royal colour, and the gay community dons tiaras, tinsel and over-the-top fancy dress. Over a million people take part.

buildings) dominate the city centre. Many of the city's famous *hofjes* – courtyards, originally built as almshouses or for religious communities – now are student housing.

Amsterdam feels almost like a big village. Most people who know the centre know each other, if only by sight, and the mayor is frequently to be seen on public transport, where he listens in on people's conversations, to find out what they care about. This village atmosphere is absorbing; if you stay a few days you are treated as an

CYCLE CITY

• First-time visitors to Amsterdam may well be mown down by a speeding bicycle within a few moments of arrival. Designated cycle paths through the city often run contrary to the traffic flow, so you have to look both ways before crossing any road. Soon you will be joining in the fun; using a Dutch 'sit-up-and-beg' bicycle without brakes – instead you have to back pedal – takes skill but soon becomes second nature. Never leave your bicycle unlocked as there is a large amount of bike theft.

honorary citizen. Amsterdammers' sociability makes it easy to get to know people – as does the fact that many speak several languages.

Intellectual, curious about the world and great talkers, it is not surprising that Amsterdammers have dared to embark on some of the great social experiments of our time. It sometimes seems that where Amsterdam, with the rest of the Netherlands, leads, the world generally follows – though maybe a few centuries later. Prostitution has been tolerated in Amsterdam

Above: NEMO (newMetropolis) the interactive museum of science and technology is also a striking piece of architecture

NEW MILLENNIUM

● In January 2001, bulldozers moved in to take up the cobbles and tram rails in front of the Royal Palace as part of a scheme to turn Dam, the city's main square, into an Italian-style piazza. The Van Gogh Museum has a striking 1999 extension of slate and glass, designed by the Japanese architect, Kisho Kurokawa. Museumplein, once a windswept car park, now has modernistic glass and steel pavilions housing museum shops and cafés. The He Wa Buddhist Temple opened in Zeedijk in September 2000, built and funded by the local Chinese community. On the waterfront is the stunning NEMO (newMetropolis) science museum, designed by Genoese architect Renzo Piano to resemble the hull of a liner, with a sweeping flight of terraced steps that takes you to the pinnacle for an unrivalled view over the city.

Above: the Tropenmuseum displays artefacts from the tropical regions of the world, giving a glimpse into the daily life of the inhabitants

TREE STORY

• Satutesque elms once lined Amsterdam's canals, but many succumbed to Dutch elm disease in the 1970s – the beetle-born fungus first identified here. Plane trees, their replacements, withstand city pollution by shedding their bark.

since the 17th century, when local officials used to make a small fortune from the sex industry. Amsterdam's liberal drug laws allow licensed cafés to permit the sale of cannabis. Amsterdam invented traffic calming – tough laws and schemes to discourage cars and improve driving conditions—and may yet become the first city to ban cars outright. Laws permit euthanasia and gay marriages. The Dutch police and military are more liberal than in many a European state, and the Dutch are passionately in favour of greater European integration. The squatter movement colonises empty buildings and draws attention to the lack of affordable housing within the city. This social liberalism is reflected in Amsterdammers' lifestyle. Informality is the norm – local business people long ago abandoned suits and ties, and restaurants are refreshingly unpretentious. Many a street corner has a *bruin kroegen* (brown café), named after the mellow hue of the tobacco-stained walls where people

Above: *Amsterdam's oldest church, Oude Kerk, is a haven of spirituality in the midst of the Red Light District*

comfortably settle down with a newspaper, or play a game of chess, or argue over the issues of the day with friends and regulars. At weekends Amsterdammers make the most of the recreational opportunities around them: flat land – perfect for cycling – and an abundance of water for swimming, sailing and watersports. People work hard when they need to, but whenever the sun shines, and in this northern latitude and maritime climate the skies more often than not hint at rain, Amsterdammers are out in the streets and enjoying their city – as will you.

THE STATE OF THE WATER

• Wandering around the city's canals you might see Ben de Rood. He's a well-known figure in Amsterdam – operating from an old tug boat with a grab crane, he has spent the last thirty years fishing rubbish out of the water. He reckons to haul up about 300 bicycles a day, and all sorts of domestic refuse. Ben is part of the city's effort to keep the canals clean. In the 1970s they were stagnant, but today the canals are flushed through regularly with fresh water from the rivers Amstel and IJ. Now they are so clean that fish and eels have returned.

DIVERSITY

• Colonial ties with the Dutch East Indies (now Indonesia) and Dutch Guyana (now Surinam) have given Amsterdam a large ethnic population, swelled by immigrants from Turkey and Morocco. Many come to shop at the colourful Albert Cuypstraat street market, jammed with foods and textiles from around the world.

15

Amsterdam Then

BEFORE 1400

Herring fisherman settle on the Amstel in the 13th century and a dam is built across the river. In 1300 the settlement is given city status and in 1345 becomes a pilgrimage centre and a major trading post although remaining very small.

HERRING CITY

If there had been no herring, Amsterdam might never have come into existence. In the Middle Ages, the Dutch discovered how to cure these fish, and they became a staple food. Herring fishermen built a dam across the Amstel river and a small fishing village developed, Amstelledamme. Its site is now Dam, Amsterdam's main square.

1425 First horseshoe canal, the Singel, is dug.

1517 Protestant Reformation in Germany. Lutheran and Calvanist ideas take root in Amsterdam.

1519 Amsterdam becomes part of the Spanish empire and nominally Catholic.

1567–68 Start of the Eighty Years' War against Spanish rule.

1578 Amsterdam capitulates to William of Orange. Calvanists take power.

17th century Dutch Golden Age. Amsterdam becomes the most important port in the world.

1602 Dutch East India Company founded.

1613 Work starts on the Gratchtengordel (Canal Ring).

1648 End of war with Spain.

1652–54 First of a series of wars with Britain for maritime supremacy.

1784 British navy destroys Dutch fleet.

1806 Napoleon Bonaparte takes over the republic.

From left to right: *map of Amsterdam, c1544; William I of Orange (1533–84); the returning fleet of the Dutch East India Company in the 17th century; Amsterdam Olympics, 1928; Anne Frank (1929–45)*

1813 Prince William returns from exile. Crowned William I in 1814.

1876 North Sea Canal opens, bringing new prosperity.

1928 Amsterdam hosts the Olympics.

1914–18 World War I. Netherlands neutral.

1940–45 German Occupation in World War II. Anne Frank goes into hiding.

1960s–70s Hippies flock to the city from all over Europe.

1964–67 Anti-establishment riots in the city.

1980 Queen Beatrix crowned. The city is named Holland's capital.

1989 City government falls because of weak anti-vehicle laws. New laws are passed to make Amsterdam eventually free of motor traffic.

1990 Van Gogh exhibition attracts 890,000 visitors.

1998–99 Redevelopment of Museumplein. A new wing is added to the Van Gogh Museum and the Rembrandthuis.

2002 Opening of Stedelijk Museum of Modern Art extension.

A POPULAR MONARCH

Beatrix, Queen of the Netherlands, came to the throne when her mother Queen Juliana, abdicated on 30 April 1980. Beatrix, born in 1938, was crowned at the Nieuwe Kerk. Her great popularity is reflected on her official birthday (*Koninginnedag*, 30 April) – an exuberantly celebrated national holiday.

Time to Shop

From flowers to fashions, clocks to souvenirs, there's plenty to see in the shop windows of Amsterdam

Amsterdam is full of fascinating quirky shops specialising in everything from toothbrushes to aboriginal art, children's comics to art-deco lamps, potted plants to exotic cut flowers, jazz CDs to cheese, beer or African masks. These shops are not always in the obvious places.

CLUMPING CLOGS

Think Amsterdam and you'll probably think of clogs – or *klompen* as they are known in Dutch, a splendidly onomatopoeic word that imitates the heavy clumping sound that wearers of the wooden shoes make as they stroll the city's pavements. They are carved from a single block of poplar wood and are extremely comfortable. Most however are sold as decorative souvenirs rather than footwear. You'll find these painted with windmills, tulips or cheeses.

Amsterdam's main shopping streets – Niewendijk and Kalverstraat – are dominated by global brands. Instead look where rents are low: along Haarlemerstraat, Daamstraat and in the cross streets of Canal Circle and the Jordaan. These cross streets were deliberately zoned for commercial use in the 17th century, when the canal circle was planned and thrived on the trade in furs and hides. Just go and wander down Reestraat, Hartenstraat, Berenstraat, Runstraat and Huidenstraat among the medley of small specialist shops, cafés and art galleries, which have replaced the original furriers.

The entrepreneurs who run these shops have a passion for their product and they want to share their enthusiasm, so customers are not treated merely as consumers, but as fellow connoisseurs. Some will happily spend all day talking about their sources. Others are busy making the products they sell – gorgeously decorated hats, Venetian-style masks, recycled vintage clothing, evening dresses or costume jewellery.

The range of specialities and what they say about human ingenuity is incredible. If it's chocolate you want, go and talk to Hendrikse, the owner of Hendrikse Le Confisuer (✉ Overtoom 448–50) who produces a wonderful range of handmade truffles as well as sculpted chocolate figures of

people and animals. Feeling guilty about consuming all that sugar? De Witte Tandenwinkel (✉ Runstraat 5) sells every imaginable colour of toothbrush and every possible flavour of toothpaste, Olivaria (✉ Hazenstraat 2A) is devoted to olive oils, De Jongejan (✉ Noorderkerkstraat 18) to eyewear – everything from vintage frames and mirrored shades to glam-rock extravaganzas. Joe's Vliergerwinkel (✉ Niewue Hoogstraat 19) sells only toys that fly – colourful kites, boomerangs and frisbees. Even the humble button gets its own emporium De Knopenwinkel (► 78), and lovers of children's and adults' comics, new and second-hand, are at Lambiek (✉ Kerkstraat 78).

You will find more flowers and bulbs in Amsterdam than any other European city – not just in the Floating Flower Market, but all around the Canal Circle. What better souvenir of your stay than a bouquet of blooms – always buy blooms that are still closed – or a packet of bulbs, but be sure to check the import regulations first.

FLEA MARKETS

The dark days of World War II engendered a habit of thrift in the citizens of Amsterdam, and even in today's relatively prosperous times, no true Amsterdammer ever throws anything away. Instead, everything – from dead light bulbs to ancient newspapers – gets recycled at one of the city's many flea markets. The biggest and best known is the one that surrounds two sides of the Stadhuis (Town Hall) on Waterlooplein. Stalls here mix the new, the old and the unimaginably decrepit. Pick up very serviceable second-hand clothes, craft items and jewellery, and wonder why anyone would want to buy a broken radio, chipped vase or a doll without a head. Other flea markets: De Looier, Rommelmarkt and Noordermarket.

Out and About

SIGHTSEEING TOURS

LAND TOURS
Holland International
✉ Prins Hendrikkade 33a
☎ 6227788. Cruises
every 15 mins in summer;
every 30 mins in winter.
Canal Bus Tours
✉ Weteingschans 24
☎ 6239886. Water-bus
service around the city.
Museumboat
✉ Stationsplein 8
☎ 6222181. Links six
jetties near the 20 major
museums. Service every
30–45 mins.

WATER TOURS
Yellow Bike Tours
✉ Nieuwezijds Kolk 29
☎ 6206940. In town and
out.

TOURIST TRAM
✉ Centraal Station
☎ 0900/9292. Explore
the Red Light District.

AIR TOURS
KLM Helicopter Tours
✉ Schiphol Airport
☎ 4747747

ITINERARIES
HISTORIC CITY
Start by visiting the Amsterdams Historisch
Museum (► 37) to get an idea of the city's
colourful history. Then stop at the Begijnhof
(► 36), Holland's finest almshouses. For lunch
try Café Esprit (► 71), a smart designer café
popular with shoppers, or a Dutch restaurant,
such as Haesje Claes (► 64). After lunch enjoy
the street entertainment between visits to the
sumptuous Koninklijk Paleis (Royal Palace
► 38) and Nieuwe Kerk (► 39), both on the
dam (now Dam square) that gave Amsterdam
its name. Having booked in advance, if possible,
go to a classical music concert at the
Concertgebouw (► 56 and 80) or Bours van
Berlage, or take in a performance of opera or
dance at the Muziektheater (► 57, 79 and 80).

MARITIME HISTORY
It's easy to imagine 17th-century Amsterdam at
the peak of its maritime success during an early
morning stroll around the Western islands
(► 53). A bus ride from here (nos. 22, 32) takes
you to the Eastern islands and the Scheepvaart
Museum (► 49). For lunch try the museum
restaurant. Then head for the Tropenmuseum
(► 50), which re-creates tropical scenes, or
walk to the Hortus Botanicus (► 60), the botanical gardens with more than 8,000 plant species,
beside Artis Zoo (► 61). Continue to the
Museum Willet-Holthuysen (► 44), built for a
wealthy Golden Age merchant. In the evening
take a candlelit cruise and see the Golden Age
buildings and canal bridges lit up.

EXCURSIONS
KEUKENHOF GARDENS

These gardens – whose name means kitchen gardens – at the heart of the *Bloembollenstreek* bulb-growing region rank among the most famous in the world. The site was used for market gardening until a consortium of bulb-growers realised the tourist potential of a site close to Amsterdam, and the 28ha of woodland park close to Lisse were acquired in 1949 as a showcase. Visit between March and late May, when more than seven million bulbs are in bloom, laid out in brilliant swathes of red, yellow, pink and blue. Few people leave without a bag of bulbs for their own garden.

DELFT

This charming old town is known the world over for its blue-and-white pottery. In 1652 there were 32 thriving potteries; today there is just one. Delft was also the birthplace of the artist Johannes Vermeer (1632–75). His simple grave can be seen in the Oude Kerk along with those of other eminent Delft citizens, including Antoine van Leeuwenhoek, inventor of the microscope (1632–1723).

William of Orange lead his revolt against Spanish rule from the Prinsenhof in Delft. The building now houses the city museum, which includes a collection of rare antique Delftware. Halfway up the stairs you can still see the holes made by the bullets that killed William in 1584. His marble tomb, designed by Hendrick de Keyser in 1614, lies in the Nieuwe Kerk.

From left to right:
historic barges outside NEMO museum;
the view from the city's canals;
the best time to visit Keukenhof is in the spring;
a variety of plates, vases and other articles in the unmistakable blue-glaxed Delftware

INFORMATION

KEUKENHOF
Distance 39km southwest
Travel time 1 hour
🎫 Combined rail/bus/admission tickets from Centraal Station
✉ Lisse
☎ 0252/465555

DELFT
Distance 50km southwest
Travel time 1 hour
🚉 Train from Centraal Station to The Hague then change for Delft
✉ Markt 83–85
☎ 015/2126100

Walks

INFORMATION

Distance 4km
Time 1–2 hours
Start/End point ★ Dam
⊞ G5
🚋 Tram 4, 9, 14, 16, 20, 24, 25

THE CANAL RING AND JORDAAN

Leave Dam square via Paleisstraat; continue straight on over the scenic Singel, Herengracht and Keizersgracht canals, and then turn right alongside Prinsengracht to pass the high tower of the Westerkerk and Anne Frankhuis (Anne Frank's House). Cross over Prinsengracht and double back for a few metres along the west bank of the canal until you reach the peaceful Bloemgracht canal. Turn right here, take the second right up Tweede Leliedwarsstraat, cross over Egelantiersgracht, and turn right along its shady bank and then left up Tweede Egelantiersdwarsstraat into the heart of the bohemian Jordaan district.

Walk on to Lijnbaansgracht, and then turn right on to Lindengracht, once a canal and now site of a Saturday food market, to Brouwersgracht (► 52), lined with traditional barges and house-boats. Cross Brouwersgracht at Herengracht and continue along Brouwersgracht to the Singel. Cross by the sluice gates and turn right along the eastern side of the Singel, past Amsterdam's narrowest house façade (No. 7). To conclude the walk, turn left at Torenstraat, cross Spui and go along Molensteeg. Continue across Nieuwezijds Voorburgwal, past Nieuwe Kerk on the left and return to Dam square.

Lindengracht
Brouwersgracht
Keizersgracht
Jordaan district
Herengracht

Egelantiersgracht
Singel
Anne Frankhuis
Westerkerk
Nieuwe Kerk
Prinsengracht
Dam

Koninklijk Paleis

MARKETS AND MUSEUMS

Leaving Dam square via Paleisstraat, turn left on to Nieuwezijds Voorburgwal, where a stamp and coin market is held (➤ 55). About 100 metres farther on the left, Sint Luciensteeg leads to the Amsterdams Historisch Museum. Pass through the Schuttersgalerij (Civic Guard Gallery) into a lane of whitewashed houses called Gedempte Begijnensloot. At the southern end, a stone archway on your right brings you into the leafy, cobbled, Begijnhof courtyard. A further archway leads to Spui and its pavement cafés. On Fridays, stalls sell antiquarian books, and on Sundays paintings and prints.

Head southwest from Spui and turn left along the edge of the Singel. Cross the bridge on to Koningsplein and Amsterdam's flower market, the Bloemenmarkt. Your next landmark is the Munttoren at Muntplein. Turn right and follow the Amstel just past the Blauwbrug (Blue Bridge). Turn right along Herengracht for a short detour to the Willet-Holthuysen Museum, an elegant patrician mansion. On your return, cross the bridge to reach the Waterlooplein flea market. Tucked away at the far end of the market is the Museum het Rembrandthuis which is not to be missed. After your walk have a drink on the terrace of Café Dantzig (➤ 70).

INFORMATION

Distance 2.5km
Time 1–2 hours
Start point ★ Dam
🚌 G5
🚊 Tram 4, 9, 14, 16, 20, 24, 25
End point Museum het Rembrandthuis
🚌 J7
Ⓜ Waterlooplein

0   1 km

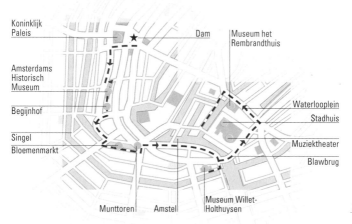

Amsterdam by Night

Above: *the Concertgebouw, built in 1888, looks beautiful illuminated at night.*
Above right: *café-club in Rembrandtplein*

CITY OF JAZZ

Amsterdam's theme tune is the wail of a jazz saxophone mingling with the keening of seagulls. This is a city that adores jazz and blues, and there are scores of venues to chose from, including the legendary BIMhaus and Maloe Melo. Not content to rock every day, the city also hosts the International Blues Festival in mid-March (www.meervaart.nl), and the North Sea Jazz Festival in mid-July (www.northseajazz.nl). Both have the kind of status that attracts huge international stars with cult performers – and aficionados flock from all over Europe to hear them.

Amsterdam is one of Europe's most vibrant nightlife capitals. On a mild summer's evening nothing beats just walking by the canal, or gliding along the canals in a glass-bottomed boat, to see the historic bridges and buildings spotlighted or outlined in white lights. Alternatively sit out of doors to enjoy a drink at a canalside café or stop at a brown café or two (➤ 82). For those who prefer a romantic dinner the choice is tremendous, with Indonesian cuisine a favourite.

There is plenty going on at the cinemas, both mainstream and art house. Don't miss the Tuschinski Theater (➤ 79). It is a splendid elaborate art-deco style building, and for the priciest tickets you get a glass of champagne included.

If you book in advance, you can hear some of the world's leading orchestras (➤ 80). Even if you don't plan ahead, there is always something going on – many churches host choral concerts and organ recitals, and the Milkweg and Paradiso nightclubs have rock and pop, the BIMhuis has jazz and Maloe Melo (➤ 81) has blues and rock.

Amsterdam nightclubs offer every kind of entertainment, including plenty that is explicitly erotic in the Red Light District. Leidesplein and Rembrandtplein throng with people out for a pre-party drink; they head for Escape (✉ Rembrandtplein 11), one of Europe's biggest and best-known clubs, or iT (✉ Amstelstraat 24), where beautiful people either wear as few clothes as possible or dress up like actors in a Fellini film. Look at the pictures outside to get an idea of what goes on.

AMSTERDAM's
top 25 sights

The sights are shown on the maps on the inside front cover and inside back cover, numbered **1**–**25** across the city

Vondelpark

Open-air auditorium in Vondelpark

This is a favourite place for sunbathers, joggers, frisbee-throwers and book-worms – great for people-watching. Be entertained by musicians, mime artists and acrobats in this welcome splash of green near the city centre.

Pleasure gardens Amsterdam's largest and oldest municipal park – a 48-ha rectangle of former marshland – was first opened in 1865. The designers, J D and L P Zocher, intentionally moved away from the symmetrical Dutch garden, creating in the romantic English style with lengthy pathways, open lawns, ornamental lakes, meadows and woodland containing 120 varieties of tree, including catalpa, chestnut, cypress, oak and poplar. Financed by wealthy local residents, the Nieuwe Park (as it was then called) became the heart of a luxurious new residential district, overlooked by elegant town houses and villas. Two years later, a statue of Holland's best-known playwright, Joost van den Vondel (1587–1679) – a Dutch contemporary of Shakespeare – was erected in the park and its present name was adopted. Today, with its wide open spaces, fragrant rose garden, playgrounds, bandstand and teahouses, it remains a popular destination for family outings. It is the only city park in Holland which has been designated a listed monument. It also has the Nederlands Filmmuseum, an absolute must for cinephiles.

Like a summer-long pop festival The heyday of the Vondelpark was in the 1970s, when hippies flocked to Amsterdam, attracted by the city's tolerance for soft drugs. Vondelpark soon became their main gathering place. The bubble burst at the end of the decade and the hippies dispersed. All that now remains are street musicians, fl markets and the occasional ageing hippy.

Stedelijk Museum

One of the world's leading modern art museums. From Henri Matisse to Kazimir Malevich and Piet Mondrian, from Paul Klee to Vasily Kandinsky and Edward Keinholz, this gallery is an essential stop for art enthusiasts.

Controversial The Stedelijk or Municipal Museum, Amsterdam's foremost venue for contemporary art, was founded in 1895. Its collection of over 25,000 paintings, sculptures, drawings, graphics and photographs contains works by some of the great names of modern art (van Gogh, Cézanne, Picasso, Monet, Chagall), but the main emphasis is on progressive postwar movements and the exhibitions highlight the very latest, often highly controversial, trends in contemporary art. There is not enough space to keep the entire collection on view, but an extension is planned to open around 2002.

House of Museums In 1938 the Stedelijk became Holland's National Museum of Modern Art, but it achieved its worldwide avant-garde reputation in 1945–63, when it was under the dynamic direction of Willem Sandberg. He put much of its existing collection in storage and created a House of Museums in which art, photography, dance, theatre, music and cinema were all represented in innovative shows.

Cutting edge Museum highlights include suprematist paintings by Malevich; works by Mondrian, Gerrit Rietveld and other exponents of the Dutch *De Stijl* school; and a remarkable collection of almost childlike paintings by the *CoBrA* movement, founded in defiance of the artistic complacency of postwar Europe, and named after the native cities of its members – Copenhagen, Brussels and Amsterdam.

HIGHLIGHTS

- *The Parakeet and the Mermaid,* Matisse (1952–3)
- *The Women of the Revolution,* Kiefer (1986)
- *My Name as Though it were Written on the Surface of the Moon,* Nauman (1986)
- *Sitting Woman with Fish Hat,* Picasso (1942)
- *The Appelbar,* Appel (1951)
- *Beanery,* Kienholz (1965)
- Rietveld furniture collection

INFORMATION

- C11; Locator map A4
- Paulus Potterstraat 13
- 5732911; www.stedelijk.nl
- Daily 11–5
- Restaurant
- Tram 2, 3, 5, 12, 16, 20; bus 63
- Museumboat stop 3
- Very good
- Moderate
- Vondelpark (➤ 26), Van Gogh Museum (➤ 28), Rijksmuseum (➤ 30)
- Lectures, films and concerts

Top: special exhibitions are a feature of the Stedelijk Museum

Van Gogh Museum

HIGHLIGHTS

- *The Potato Eaters* (1885)
- *Bedroom at Arles* (1888)
- *Vase with Sunflowers* (1888)
- *Wheatfield with Crows* (1890)

DID YOU KNOW?

- Van Gogh sold only one painting in his lifetime
- Record price for a van Gogh painting is f82.5 million (1990 *Portrait of Dr Gachet*)

INFORMATION

- D11; Locator map A4
- Paulus Potterstraat 7
- 5705200; www.vangoghmuseum.nl
- Daily 10–6
- Self-service restaurant
- Tram 2, 3, 5, 12, 16, 20
- Museumboat stop 3
- Excellent
- Expensive

Top: bedroom at Arles
Below: self-portrait

It is a moving experience to trace this great artist's tragic life and extraordinary achievement, through such a wide display of his art, his Japanese prints and contemporary works.

World's largest van Gogh collection Of his 900 paintings and 1,200 drawings, the Van Gogh Museum has 200 and 500 respectively, together with 850 letters, Vincent's fine Japanese prints and works by friends and influential contemporaries, including Gauguin, Monet, Bernard and Pissarro. Van Gogh's paintings are arranged chronologically, starting with works from 1880 to 1887, a period characterised by realistic landscape paintings and peasant scenes in heavy tones. This period is typified by *The Potato Eaters* (1885).

Colourful palette The broad brush strokes and bold colours that characterise van Gogh's works of 1887–90 show the influence of his 1886 move to Paris and the effect of Impressionism, most striking in street and café scenes. Tired of city life, he moved in 1888 to Arles where, intoxicated by the intense sunlight and the brilliant colours of Provence, he painted many of his finest works, including *Harvest at La Crau* and the *Sunflowers* series. After snipping off a bit of his ear and offering it to a local prostitute, van Gogh voluntarily entered an asylum in St Remy, where his art took an expressionistic form. His mental anguish may be seen in the way he painted gnarled trees and menacing skies, as in the desolate *Wheatfield with Crows*. Shortly after completing this picture, at the age of 37, he shot himself.

Extra space In May 1999 the museum reopened after extensive renovation, and the construction of an ellipse-shaped wing designed by Japanese architect Kisho Kurokawa.

Leidseplein

This square represents Amsterdam's nightlife at its vibrant best. It is filled with pavement cafés, ablaze with neon and a-buzz with jugglers, acrobats, musicians and fire-eaters.

Party centre for centuries During the Middle Ages, farmers on their way to market unloaded their carts here, at the outskirts of the city. At the turn of the 19th century, artists and writers gathered here. In the 1930s Leidseplein was the site of many clashes between political factions, and it became the main site of anti-Nazi rallies during the war. In the 1960s it was the stomping ground of the *Pleiners* (Dutch Mods), and in 1992 it witnessed wild celebrations following local football team Ajax's UEFA Cup victory. Today, despite the constant flow of trams through the square, you will always find fire-eaters, sword-swallowers and other interesting street entertainment. By night, dazzling neon lights and crowded café terraces seating over 1,000 people transform the square into an Amsterdam hot spot, busy until the early hours. Be sure to spend at least one evening here. Look for two notable buildings, both protected monuments: the distinctive, attractive red-brick Stadsschouw-burg (Municipal Theater), with its wide verandah and little turrets, and the art nouveau American Hotel, with its striking art deco Café Américain.

Winter wonderland Whatever the season, Leidseplein remains one of the city's main meeting places. In winter, when most tourists have returned home, it becomes quintessentially Dutch. Most of the outdoor café terraces disappear and locals huddle together for a drink and a t in heated covered terraces, or inside the s. It is also *the* place to be on New Year's Eve.

HIGHLIGHTS

- American Hotel (1904)
- Stadsschouwburg (1894)
- Street entertainment

INFORMATION

- D9; Locator map B3
- Leidseplein
- Restaurants and cafés
- Tram 1, 2, 5, 6, 7, 10, 20
- Museumboat stop 3
- Vondelpark (➤ 26), Rijksmuseum (➤ 30), Prinsengracht (➤ 31)

Top: cafés in Leidseplein by night. Below: a stilt walker entertains

Rijksmuseum

HIGHLIGHTS

- *The Night Watch,* Rembrandt (1642)
- *The Milk Maid,* Vermeer
- *Flower Piece,* Jan Brueghel
- *Winter Landscape with Iceskaters,* Hendrick Avercamp
- *The Merry Family,* Jan Steen

INFORMATION

- ✠ E10; Locator map B4
- ✉ Stadhouderskade 42
- ☎ 6747047; www.rijksmuseum.nl
- 🕐 Daily 10–5
- 🍴 Café/restaurant
- 🚊 Tram 2, 5, 6, 7, 10, 20
- Museumboat stop 3
- ♿ Very good
- 💷 Expensive
- ❓ Audio-tour; interactive centre

Top: The Merry Family, *Jan Steen. Below:* self-portrait as the Apostle Paul, *Rembrandt*

Holland's biggest museum has a mind-numbing seven million items in its catalogue, ranging from the world's most important collection of Dutch Golden Age masterpieces to model sailing ships and doll's houses.

Masterpieces Housed in a palatial red-brick building designed by P J H Cuypers and opened in 1885, the Rijksmuseum boasts an unrivalled collection of Old Master paintings in more than 250 rooms, a library with 250,000 volumes, a million prints and drawings and thousands of sculptures and other artefacts. The museum's ground floor traces the course of Dutch painting from religious pieces of the medieval era to the rich paintings of the Renaissance and the Golden Age, including works by Rembrandt, Vermeer, Hals and Steen. Pride of place goes to Rembrandt's *The Night Watch* (1642). This vast, dramatic canvas – one of his largest and most famous compositions, portraying a militia company – is a showpiece of 17th-century Dutch art. It was originally even bigger, but Rembrandt cut it down considerably, reputedly to get it through a doorway. Displayed in the adjacent room is a copy of *The Night Watch* attributed to Lundens, in the original form.

Treasures Along with the remarkable Dutch paintings, the museum's riches include a collection of Delftware and Meissen porcelain, countless sculptures and Asian treasures, a fascinating section on Dutch history, and two ingeniously made doll's houses – scaled-down copies of old canal houses with sumptuous 17th-century period furnishings. The refurbished south win of the museum contains a magnificent collecti of Dutch Romantic works and Impressio paintings by local artists.

Prinsengracht

Of the three canals that form the Grachtengordel (Canal Ring), Prinsengracht is in many ways the most atmospheric, with its fine merchants' homes, converted warehouses and flower-laden houseboats.

Prince William's canal Prinsengracht (Prince's Canal), named after William of Orange, was dug at the same time as Herengracht and Keizersgracht as part of a massive 17th-century expansion scheme. Together these three form the city's distinctive horseshoe-shaped canal network. Less exclusive than the other two waterways, with smaller houses, Prinsengracht became an important thoroughfare lined with warehouses and merchants' homes. Cargo would be unloaded from ships into fourth-floor storehouses by means of the massive hoist-beams seen today in the gables of many buildings (and still used for lifting furniture). Some houses were built with a deliberate tilt, to protect their façades from the goods as they were hoisted.

Floating homes Today, you'll also see some of Amsterdam's most beautiful houseboats moored along Prinsengracht, near Brouwersgracht and alongside the ivy-covered quays close to the Amstel. Amsterdammers have long lived in houseboats, but the housing crisis after World War II skyrocketed the population of boat-people, so that there are more than 2,500 legal houseboats in Amsterdam, all with a postal address and power hook-ups. The unofficial figure is a lot higher. You can see a variety of craft on Prinsengracht, some more seaworthy than others, ranging from solid old Rhine barges to chalet-like rafts, boats with greenhouses and gardens and trendy studio homes.

HIGHLIGHTS

- Amstelkerk (► 59)
- Anne Frankhuis (► 33)
- Noorderkerk (► 59)
- Noordermarkt (► 55)
- Westerkerk (► 32)

DID YOU KNOW?

- Prinsengracht is 4.5km long, 2m deep and 25m wide to accommodate four lanes of shipping
- A law (dating from 1565) restricts the lean of canal houses to 1:25

INFORMATION

- ✚ E3–J10; Locator map B2
- 🍴 Bars, cafés, restaurants
- 🚋 Tram 1, 2, 4, 5, 13, 14, 16, 17, 20, 24, 25
- 🛥 Museumboat stop 2
- ↔ Herengracht (► 34), Anne Frankhuis (► 33),Westerkerk (► 32)

31

Westerkerk

HIGHLIGHTS

- Climbing the tower
- Organ, Johannes Duyschot (1686)
- Anne Frank statue, Mari Andriessen
- Rembrandt memorial column
- Grave of Rembrandt's son, Titus

DID YOU KNOW?

- The church was consecrated in 1631
- The tower contains 48 bells
- The largest bell weighs 7,500kg and its hammer weight is 200kg

INFORMATION

- D5; Locator map B2
- Prinsengracht 281, Westermarkt
- 6247766
- Church Mon–Fri 11-3. Tower Apr–Sep: ·Mon–Fri 10–5
- Tram 13, 14, 17, 20
- Museumboat stop 2
- Few
- Inexpensive (tower)
- Prinsengracht (► 31), Anne Frankhuis (► 33)
- Carillon concerts most Tue at noon

This is the most beautiful of the four churches built in the 17th century to the north, south, east and west of the city centre. The views from the tall tower are unsurpassable and make the 85-m climb worthwhile.

Masterwork The West Church, the church most visited by tourists in the city, has the largest nave of any Dutch Protestant church, and the tallest tower and largest congregation in Amsterdam. It is the masterwork of Dutch architect Hendrick de Keyser, who died in 1621, one year after construction began. Designed to serve the wealthy bourgeoisie living in the stylish new mansions of the Canal Ring, it was eventually completed by his son Pieter with Cornelis Dancker in 1631. To its tower they added the gaudy golden crown – a symbol of the city granted by Habsburg Emperor Maximilian 150 years earlier. The sweeping views over the Prinsengracht gables can be seen from the tower, popularly called 'Lange Jan' (Tall John). Outside the church, people often lay wreaths at the foot of the statue of Anne Frank (► 33), who used to listen to the church bells while she was in hiding, before the bells were melted down by the Nazis.

Interior The simple, whitewashed interior is laid out in the shape of a double Greek cross. The massive organ is decorated with musical instruments and frescos of the Evangelists by Gerard de Lairesse, who was one of Rembrandt's pupils. Rembrandt himself was buried here on 8 October 1669. Although no trace of his pauper's grave remains, there is a memorial to him in the north aisle, near the grave of his son, Titus. The church's opening hours for visitors are not guaranteed; it may be closed at the times stated.

Anne Frankhuis

'My greatest wish is to be a journalist, and later on, a famous writer... I'd like to publish a book called 'The Secret Annexe'. It remains to be seen whether I'll succeed, but my diary can serve as a basis.'

Unfulfilled wish On Thursday 11 May 1944, just under three months before she was captured by the Nazis, Anne Frank wrote these poignant words in her diary. She never saw it published, but died in the concentration camp at Belsen near the end of World War II, at the age of 15.

'The Secret Annexe' After Nazi Germany invaded the Netherlands in 1940, increasingly severe anti-Semitic measures were introduced. In 1942, the Frank and van Daan families went into hiding. For the next two years, Anne Frank kept a diary describing daily life and the families' isolation and fear of discovery – until they were betrayed to the Nazis in 1944. Her father was the only member of the group to survive. In 1947, following her wishes, he published her diary, calling it *Het Achterhuis* (The Secret Annexe). Today, over half a million visitors annually make their way through the revolving bookcase that conceals the entrance into the small, gloomy rooms so vividly described in the diary. Mementos on the walls include a map showing the Allied armies' advance from Normandy. Pencilled lines mark the children's growth. The building is preserved by the Anne Frank Foundation, an organisation founded to combat racism and anti-Semitism and to promote 'the ideals set down in the Diary of Anne Frank'. In one entry Anne wrote: 'I want to go on living even after my death!' Thanks to her diary, this wish, at least, came true.

HIGHLIGHTS

- The Nazis occupied Amsterdam for five years
- Of Holland's 140,000 pre-war Jewish population only 16,000 survived

INFORMATION

- E4; Locator map B2
- Prinsengracht 263
- 5567100; www.annefrank.nl
- Sep–Mar: daily 9–7. Apr–Aug: daily 9–9. 25 Dec, 1Jan noon–7
- Tram 13, 14, 17, 20
- Museumboat stop 2
- None
- Expensive
- 5-minute introductory film

Top: the revolving bookcase. Below: sculpture of Anne Frank

Herengracht

INFORMATION

DID YOU KNOW?

- If you stand on the bridge at the junction of Herengracht and Reguhersgracht, you can see 15 bridges simutaneously

Top: a bell gable beside the Herengracht

Exploring the city's grandest canal is like going back through time to Amsterdam's Golden Age. These gilded houses are a case study of four centuries of Dutch architectural styles.

The Gentlemen's Canal Herengracht takes its name from the rich merchants and traders of Amsterdam's heyday, and was the first of three concentric canals dug early in the 17th century to house the city's fast-growing population. Attracting the wealthiest merchant aristocrats, it has the largest, most ostentatious houses, 400 of which are now protected monuments. The houses had to conform to many building standards. Even the colour of the front doors – known as Amsterdam green – was regulated. Taxes were levied according to the width of the canal frontage, hence the rows of tall, narrow residences.

Gable-spotting Canal house-owners expressed themselves in the elaborate decoration of their houses' gables and façades, and you can find every imaginable design along Herengracht. The earliest and most common are the *step* gable and the *spout* gable. Amsterdam's first *neck* gable (No. 168) was built in 1638 by Philip Vingboons, and the *bell* gable became popular early in the 18th century. Around this time, Louis XIV-style façades were considered the height of fashion. Number 475 is a fine example – nicknamed the jewel of canal houses.

The Golden Bend Amsterdam's most extravagant mansions, with double fronts, were built between Leidsestraat and Vijzelstraat, along the stretch of the canal since dubbed the 'Golden Bend'. To this day, it remains the most prestigious address in town.

Singel

At first glance, this canal looks like any other major waterway in the city. Look a little closer, though, and you will discover some of Amsterdam's most unusual and enchanting sights.

Former city belt From its construction in the early 15th century until the late 16th century, the city limits were marked by the Singel (originally *Cingle*, meaning belt), the city's defensive moat. Then, in 1586, the city council decided to build quays along the Singel's west bank and to convert the moat into a canal for large freight ships. Thus the Singel became the first of Amsterdam's concentric canals, and its curved shape established the horseshoe layout of the city. With the coming of the railways, canal transport became less important and the Singel began to acquire a more residential character. Many warehouses are now converted into homes. The Nieuwe Haarlemmersluis, at the junction of Singel and Brouwersgracht, is opened nightly to top up the city's canals.

Flowers and floating felines Perhaps the most unusual house is No. 7. The narrowest house in Amsterdam, it was made no wider than a front door in order to minimise property taxes (➤ 34). Opposite is the *Poezenboot*, a houseboat that is a refuge for stray cats. Look out, too, for the Torensluis (Tower Lock, on the Singel's widest bridge); in the 17th century it was used as a prison. The bridge has a monument to Multatuli (1820–87), one of the Netherlands' greatest writers. Europe's only floating flower market, the Bloemenmarkt, is also on the Singel.

HIGHLIGHTS

- Poezenboot
- Bloemenmarkt (➤ 40)
- Torensluis prison cell
- Munttoren (➤ 57)
- No. 7: narrowest house façade
- No. 2, 36, 74, 83: unusual façades

INFORMATION

- ✚ G3 F0, Locator map C2
- ✉ Singel
- ⊙ Poezenboot: 1–3PM daily
- 🍴 Cafés and restaurants
- 🚋 Tram 1, 2, 5, 13, 14, 17, 20
- 🚢 Museumboat stop 4
- ♿ Poezenboot: none
- 💵 Poezenboot: free
- ↔ Bloemenmarkt (➤ 40), Herengracht (➤ 34), Koninklijk Paleis (➤ 38), Begijnhof (➤ 36)

The Bloemenmarkt brings a riot of colour to the Singel

Begijnhof

Below: one of Amsterdam's oldest buildings, the Wooden House

Tranquillity characterises Amsterdam's many *hofjes* (almshouses), none more so than this leafy oasis. The cobbled courtyard, with houses resembling doll's houses, looks like a film set.

Pious women A tiny, unlikely looking gateway leads to the Begijnhof, the oldest and finest *hofje* in the country (almshouses were charitable lodgings for the poor). This secluded community of magnificently restored old houses and gardens clustered around a small church lies a stone's throw from the main shopping thoroughfare. It was built in 1346 as a sanctuary for the *Begijnen* or Beguines, unmarried women who wanted to live in a religious community without becoming nuns. In return for modest lodging, they devoted themselves to the care of the poor and sick. Today, the Begijnhof is a residence for single women earning less than f35,000 ($18,500) a year, and has a five-year waiting list.

Two churches The Begijnkerk (1419), which dominates the courtyard, was confiscated from the Beguines during the Alteration in 1578. The women continued to worship secretly until religious tolerance was restored over 200 years later, in 1795. Meanwhile, their precious church became a warehouse until 1607, when it was given to the Presbyterian community and renamed the Engelse Kerk (English Church). The simple interior contains pulpit panels designed by Piet Mondrian. Nearby, het Houten Huys (the Wooden House, 1477) is one of only two remaining wood-fronted houses in Amsterdam. It was built before 1521, when the use of wood as a building material was banned, following a series of fires. Look out for a nearby courtyard, with walls dotted with gable stones salvaged from demolished Begijnhof houses.

Amsterdams Historisch Museum

Do make this lively and informative museum your first port of call. Once you have a grasp of Amsterdam's colourful history, walks around town are all the more rewarding.

The building This excellent museum traces the growth of Amsterdam from 13th-century fishing village to bustling metropolis, through an impressive collection of paintings, maps, models and historical artefacts. They are displayed chronologically in one of the city's oldest buildings. Originally a monastery, it was occupied by the city orphanage (Burger-weeshuis) for nearly 400 years, until 1975, when it was converted into a museum. Most of the present structure dates from the 16th and 17th centuries. Throughout, you can still see evidence of its former use – notably the ceiling paintings in the Regent's Chamber and the numerous portraits of children, including Jan Carel van Speyck, who later became a Dutch naval hero.

The collections The first rooms of the museum chronicle the city's early history and its rise to prominence in trade and commerce. The displays include furniture, memorabilia and a map that illuminates each 25-year period of growth through the centuries. The museum's main focus is on the Golden Age and colonial expansion. Paintings and photographs illustrate the growing welfare problems of the 19th and early 20th centuries, and a small collection of relics from World War II shows how the Nazi occupation affected the city's population, 10 per cent of which was Jewish. A section focuses on the 'Modern City' and finally, in the adjoining Schuttersgalerij, don't miss the portraits of the dapper Civic Guard, an armed civilian force formed in the late 14th century to police the city.

HIGHLIGHTS

- *View of Amsterdam,* Cornelis Anthonisz (1538), the oldest city map
- *The Meal of the 17 Guardsmen of Company H,* Cornelis Anthonisz (1533), in the Schuttersgalerij
- *The First Steamship on the IJ,* Nicolaas Bauo (1816)
- *Governesses at the Burgher Orphanage,* Adriaen Backer (1683)
- *Girls from the Civic Orphanage,* Nicolaas van der Waay (1880)
- Bell room

INFORMATION

- ✚ F6; Localur map C3
- ✉ Kalverstraat 92, Nieuwezijds Voorburgwal 357
- ☎ 5231822; www.ahm.nl
- 🕐 Mon–Fri 10–5; Sat, Sun 11–5. Closed 1 Jan, 30 Apr, 25 Dec
- 🍴 David and Goliath Café
- 🚊 Tram 1, 2, 4, 5, 9, 14, 16, 20, 24, 25
- ♿ Good
- ⛴ Museumboat stop 4
- 💰 Expensive
- ↔ Koninklijk Paleis (➤ 38)
- ❓ Guided tours on request: telephone in advance

Top: armour on display in the Amsterdams Historisch Museum

37

Koninklijk Paleis

HIGHLIGHTS

- Views of Dam square
- Tribunal
- Citizen's Hall
- Façade

DID YOU KNOW?

- The state bought the palace in 1936 for f10 million
- The palace rests on 13,659 piles driven 18m into the ground
- It is 80m long and 56m wide
- The bell tower is 51m high

INFORMATION

- F5; Locator map C2
- Dam
- 6204060; www.kon-paleisamsterdam.nl
- Usually Tue–Thu 12:30–5 but varies depending on state functions; phone for details.
  Closed public hols and when the Queen is in residence
- Tram 4, 9, 14, 16, 20, 24, 25
- Good
- Moderate
- Nieuwe Kerk (► 39), Amsterdams Historisch Museum (► 37), Begijnhof (► 36)

Don't be put off by the Royal Palace's sober exterior. It belies the lavish decoration inside – a reminder of the power of Amsterdam in its heyday.

Civic pride At the height of the Golden Age, architect Jacob van Campen was commissioned to design Europe's largest and grandest town hall, and its classical design was a startling and progressive departure from the Dutch Renaissance style. The poet Constantyn Huygens called the Stadhuis 'the world's Eighth Wonder' and to this day it remains the city's only secular building on such a grand scale. Note the façade's astonishing wealth of decoration, numerous statues, an elaborate pediment and a huge cupola crowned by a galleon weather vane. During the seven years of construction, a heated argument developed as to whether a tower for the Nieuwe Kerk should have priority over a town hall. This was resolved when the old town hall burned down, and in 1655 the mayor moved into his new building.

Palatial splendour The town hall was transformed into a royal palace in 1808 after Napoleon made his brother Louis King of Holland. Today it serves as an occasional residence for Queen Beatrix, whose principal palace is in The Hague. Inside, be sure to see the Tribunal and the sumptuous Burgerzaal (Citizen's Hall), running the length of the palace, with the entire eastern and western hemispheres mapped out on the floor. The Tribunal was once, the city's main courtroom, and condemned prisoners were taken from here to be hanged publicly in Dam square. The graceful Schepenzaal (Council Chamber), where the city aldermen met, has Rembrandt pupil Ferdinand Bol's painting of *Moses the Lawgiver*.

Nieuwe Kerk

Considering its turbulent history, it is something of a miracle that Holland's magnificent national church has survived. Hearing its organ is a real treat.

Not so new The 'New' Church actually dates from the 15th century, when Amsterdam was growing at such a rate that the 'Old' Church (Oude Kerk, ▶ 42) was no longer sufficient. Construction started in 1408 but the church was several times destroyed by fire. After the Alteration in 1578, (when Amsterdam officially became Protestant), and a further fire in 1645, the church was rebuilt and reconsecrated in 1648. It has no spire: following years of fierce debate, the money designated for its construction was spent to complete the Koninklijk Paleis (▶ 38). It does have one of the finest of Amsterdam's 42 historic church organs – a Schonat-Hagerbeer organ, dating from 1650–73, with 5,005 pipes and a full-voiced sound that easily fills the church's vast interior.

Famous names At the time of the Alteration, Amsterdam's churches were largely stripped of their treasures, and the Nieuwe Kerk was no exception. The altar space has since been occupied by the tomb of Holland's most valiant naval hero, Admiral Michiel de Ruyter, one of many names from Dutch history, including poets Peter Cornelisz Hooft and Joost van den Vondel, buried in the church. A window dated 1650 shows the granting of the city's coat of arms by William IV. Another, by Otto Mengelberg to mark her 40th year as queen, shows Wilhelmina at her inauguration in 1898. Dutch monarchs have been inaugurated here, from William I in 1815 to Beatrix in 1980. Although it is no longer a place of worship, it holds regular exhibitions and organ recitals.

Top: tomb of Michiel de Ruyter. Above: the Nieuwe Kerk from Dam Square

HIGHLIGHTS

- Organ, Hans Schonat and Jacob Hagerbeer (1650–73)
- Organ case, Jacob van Campen (1645)
- Pulpit, Albert Vinckenbrinck (1644)
- Tomb of Admiral de Ruyter, Rombout Verhulst (1681)

INFORMATION

- F5; Locator map C2
- Dam
- 6268168
- Usually daily 10–6
- Nieuwe Café
- Tram 1, 2, 5, 13, 14, 17, 20
- Good
- Varies with exhibitions

Bloemenmarkt

HIGHLIGHTS

- De Tuin bulb stall
  (opposite Singel 502)
  (➤ 73)
- Van Zoomeren cactus
  display (opposite Singel
  526)
- Vazoplant pots and stalls
  (opposite Singel 514)

INFORMATION

- ✚ F8; Locator map C3
- ✉ Singel (between Muntplein
  and Koningsplein)
- 🕐 Mon–Sat 9:30–5
- 🚇 Muntplein
- 🚊 Tram 1, 2, 4, 5, 9, 14, 16,
  20, 24, 25
- 🚢 Museumboat stop 4
- ♿ Good

Tulipa Whittalli *from
Curtis's Botanical
Magazine c1795*

Golden sunflowers, deep blue irises, delicately scented roses and row upon row of tulips and tulip bulbs – the barges that serve as stalls for Amsterdam's flower market are ablaze with colour, whatever the season.

Floating market During the 17th and 18th centuries there were approximately 20 floating markets in Amsterdam, at least two of which gratified the Dutch passion for tulips. Nurserymen would sail up the Amstel from their smallholdings and moor here to sell their wares directly from their boats. Today, the stalls at this, the city's only remaining floating market, are permanently moored. Offering a vast variety of seasonal flowers, plants, pots, shrubs and herbs, they are supplied by the florists of Aalsmeer and the region around Haarlem, at the horticultural heart of Holland. With over 16,000ha of the country devoted to bulb growing, it is easy to see why the Dutch are nicknamed 'the florists of Europe'.

Tulip mania Tulips were first spotted in Turkey by Dutch diplomats, who brought them back to Holland around 1600. Shortly afterwards, a Leiden botanist discovered ways of changing their shape and colour, and tulip cultivation rapidly became a national obsession. Prices soared, with single bulbs fetching up to f3,000 (an average worker's annual salary was f150). Some were even exchanged for houses, and an abundance of still life paintings was produced to capture prize blooms on canvas. In 1637, the bubble burst, and many people lost entire fortunes. Prices are more realistic today and tulip bulbs are popular souvenirs for tourists. The Bloemenmarkt remains the best place to buy the many varieties.

Rosse Buurt

Amsterdam's Red Light District, bathed in a lurid red neon glow, and full of gaping tourists, junkies and pickpockets, is one of the city's greatest attractions. Among the sleaziness, everyday life carries on regardless.

Sex for sale Because of the port and its sailor population, sex is, and long has been, big business in Amsterdam. As early as the 15th century, Amsterdam was infamous as a centre of prostitution, and the lure of the Red Light District proves irresistible to most visitors to the city today. Crowds clog the narrow alleyways, sex shops, peep shows and suggestively named bars, while bored prostitutes beckon from their pink-lit windows. But there is more to the Red Light District than sex. 'Normal' people live here, too, and go about their everyday business in what, behind the tawdry façade, is an interesting part of the old city.

Drug central The Red Light District is also frequented by drug dealers, and here you will find the great majority of Amsterdam's psychedelic, marijuana-selling 'smoking' coffee shops (► 71). The Hash Marihuana Hemp Museum on Oudezijds Achterburgwal is the only museum in Europe tracing the history of hashish and the cannabis plant, and is next to the world's only Cannabis Connoisseurs' Club.

Precautions Watch your wallet, avoid eye contact with any undesirable characters, do not take photographs of prostitutes and avoid poorly lit alleyways. Even though the evening is the liveliest time to visit, it is best not to wander around alone. Stay alert in the Red Light District and exercise caution in quiet areas at night, or avoid them completely.

DID YOU KNOW?

- Possession of drugs is technically illegal but the authorities tolerate possession of up to 30g of soft drugs (cannabis, hashish and marijuana) for personal use
- Drug-dealing is not allowed. 'Smoking' coffee shops are tolerated (► 71)
- There are 900 'coffee shops' (► 71) and 250 cannabis 'grow shops' in Holland, and around 30,000 'home-growers'.
- Brothels were legalised in 1990
- Half of Amsterdam's prostitutes are foreign

INFORMATION

- ✚ H4–H5; Locator map C2
- ✉ Borders roughly denoted by Zeedijk (north), Kloveniersburgwal (east), Damstraat (south) and Warmoesstraat (west)
- 🍴 Restaurants, bars, cafés
- 🚇 Centraal Station, Nieuwmarkt
- 🚋 Tram 4, 9, 14, 16, 20, 24, 25
- 🔁 Oude Kerk (► 42), Museum Amstelkring (► 43)

Oude Kerk

HIGHLIGHTS

- Great Organ, Vatermüller
- Stained-glass windows, Lambert van Noórt (1555)
- Carillon, F Hemony (1658)

INFORMATION

- ✚ H5; Locator map C2
- ✉ Oudekerksplein 1
- ☎ 6258284; www.oudekerk.nl
- ◷ Mon–Sat 11–5; Sun 1–5. Closed 1 Jan, 25 Dec
- 🚋 Tram 4, 9, 16, 20, 24, 25
- ♿ Good
- 🚻 Moderate
- ↔ Rosse Buurt (➤ 41)
- ❓ Frequent organ recitals and carillon concerts

The 18th-century Great Organ

Surrounded by cafés, bars and sex shops, the Old Church represents an island of spirituality in the Red Light District. Here brashness and purity rub shoulders.

History Amsterdam's oldest church, dedicated to St Nicholas, the patron saint of seafarers, was built in 1306 to replace a wooden chapel that probably dated from the late 1200s. Over the centuries the church escaped the great fires that devastated so much of the city, and the imposing basilica you see today dates largely from the 14th century. Its graceful tower, added in 1565–67, contains one of the finest carillons in Holland. In the 16th century Jan Pieters Sweelinck, Holland's best-known composer, was organist here.

Miracle In the 14th century, the Oude Kerk became one of Europe's pilgrimage centres following a miracle: communion bread regurgitated by a dying man and thrown on the fire, would not burn, and the sick man did not die. Thousands of Catholics still take part in the annual *Stille Omgang*, a silent nocturnal procession, but as the Oude Kerk is now Protestant, it no longer follows the ancient pilgrim route to the church, going instead to the Begijnhof.

Sober interior The stark, impressive interior has a triple nave and elaborate vaulting. Three magnificent windows in the Lady Chapel survived the Alteration, as did the finely carved choir stools. In the 1960s some delicate 14th-century paintings were found behind layers of blue paint in the vaults. The tombstone of Rembrandt's first wife, Saskia van Uylenburg, is still in the church even though poverty drove him to sell her grave plot.

Museum Amstelkring

Not only is this tiny museum one of the city's most surprising, it is also off the beaten tourist track, tucked away in a small, inconspicuous canal house on the edge of the Red Light District.

Best-kept secret In 1578, when the Roman Catholic city council was replaced by a Protestant one Roman Catholic churches were closed throughout the city. In 1661, while Catholic church services were still forbidden, a wealthy merchant named Jan Hartman built a residence on the Oudezijds Voorburgwal, and two adjoining houses in the Heintje Hoecks-steeg. He ran a sock shop on the ground floor, lived upstairs, rented out the spare rooms in the buildings behind and cleverly converted the top two storeys of the canal house, and the attics of all three buildings, into a secret Catholic church. Religious freedom only returned with the French occupation of the Netherlands in 1795.

Hidden church This 'schuilkerk' was just one of many clandestine churches that sprang up throughout the city, but it is the only one that has been completely preserved. It was saved from demolition in 1888 by a group of historians called the Amstelkring (Amstel circle), who nicknamed the church 'Our Dear Lord in the Attic'. To find a three-storey, galleried church at the top of a series of increasingly steep staircases is an awesome experience. With seating for 200 people, magnificent ecclesiastical statuary, silver, paintings, a collapsible altar and a huge organ, it is hard to believe that the services held here were really secret. Look for the resident priest's tiny hidden bedroom under the stairs, and the confessional on the landing. The rest of the complex has been restored, and provides a taste of domestic life in the 17th century.

HIGHLIGHTS

- Church of 'Our Dear Lord in the Attic'
- Altar painting *The Baptism of Christ,* Jacob de Wit (1716)
- Priest's bedroom
- Confessional
- Drawing room
- Kitchen

DID YOU KNOW?

- The altarpiece is one of three paintings by Jacob de Wit, designed to be interchangeable
- The church is still a consecrated place of worship

HIGHLIGHTS

- H5; Locator map D2
- Oudezijds Voorburgwal 40
- 6246604
- Mon–Sat 10–5; Sun, public hols 1–5. Closed 1 Jan, 30 Apr
- Centraal Station
- Tram 4, 9, 16, 20, 24, 25
- Centraal Station
- Museumboat stop 1
- None
- Moderate
- Classical concerts during winter

Top: 'Our Dear Lord in the Attic'

43

Museum Willet-Holthuysen

INFORMATION

- H8; Locator map D3
- Herengracht 605
- 5231870; www.ahm.nl/willet/index.html
- Mon–Fri 10–5; Sat, Sun 11–5. Closed 1 Jan, 30 Apr and 25 Dec
- Waterlooplein
- Tram 4, 9, 14, 20
- Museumboat stop 6
- None
- Moderate
- Herengracht (➤ 34), Magere Brug (➤ 47), Joods Historisch Museum (➤ 48)

Behind the impressive façade of this gracious mansion lies a sumptuously furnished home with a delightful garden, a rare luxury in Amsterdam.

Insight This beautifully preserved house on Herengracht, Amsterdam's most elegant canal (➤ 34), was built in 1687 for Jacob Hop, a wealthy member of the city council. It changed hands many times and eventually, in 1855, came into the possession of a glass merchant named Pieter Gerard Holthuysen. On his death, it became the home of his daughter Sandra and her husband, the art-collector Abraham Willet, who together built up a valuable collection of glass, silver, ceramics and paintings. The couple bequeathed the house and its contents to the city in 1895, to be used as a museum. For many years it was visited so rarely that people joked that it was the best place for a gentleman to meet his mistress unobserved. However, following extensive restoration in the late 1990s, the museum attracts an ever increasing number of visitors, and provides a rare insight into life in the grand canal-houses in the 17th to 19th centuries.

Luxury and grandeur The rooms are lavishly decorated with inlaid wood and lacquered panelling with painted ceilings. Be sure to see the Blue Room, formerly the preserve of the gentlemen of the house, and the 17th-century kitchen, with its original plumbing. Guests would be served tea in the tiny, round Garden Room that, painted in the customary pale green, looks out over an immaculate French-style formal garden, lined with topiary and studded with statues. This is one of the city's few surviving 18th-century gardens – and is a jewel not to be missed.

Top: the Dining Room laid ready for dinner

Stoeltie Diamonds

When you tour this diamond-polishing factory, be assured there is no pressure to buy, but the dazzling jewels may well leave you mesmerised.

Diamonds are forever Amsterdam's association with diamonds dates from the 16th century, when Antwerp was taken by the Spanish and thousands of refugees fled north, including Jewish diamond cutters and the city's most prosperous Jewish merchants. Amsterdam's guild controls prevented them from entering most other trades so they soon established new businesses processing diamonds and dealing in the stones, and were thriving. By the 19th century, they were employing thousands of workers, and when vast fields of diamonds were discovered in South Africa in 1867, most of the stones were brought to Amsterdam to be cut. Amsterdam reigned as the diamond capital of the world until World War II, when most of the city's Jewish workers were deported to concentration camps. Because few returned, Antwerp regained its leadership of the world diamond market after the war, but diamonds from Amsterdam are known for their quality and outstanding workmanship.

Tour Many of Amsterdam's 24 diamond-polishing factories offer tours. Stoeltie's, which lasts about 30 minutes, includes a brief history of diamonds, their many industrial applications, how they are mined and the fine art of diamond production, a surprisingly grimy process considering the brilliant product. It is fascinating to watch the craft workers at their benches, deftly cutting, polishing, sorting and setting the glittering gems. Stoeltie Diamonds is one of five members of the Amsterdam Diamond Foundation, a symbol of quality and fair dealing, though not necessarily of modest prices.

DID YOU KNOW?

- The first records of Amsterdam's diamond industry date from 1586
- At its peak, it employed over 10,000 workers
- Only 20 per cent of diamonds are used in jewellery
- The world's largest-ever cut diamond, the Cullinan (Star of Africa) weighs 530 carats. The world's smallest-ever cut diamond has 57 facets and weighs 0.0012 carats. Both were processed in Amsterdam
- The General Dutch Diamond Workers Union, founded in 1894, was the first union in the world to win an eight-hour working day

INFORMATION

- ✚ H8; Locator map D3
- ✉ Wagenstraat 13–17
- ☎ 6237601
- 🕐 Daily 8:30–5
- 🚇 Waterlooplein
- 🚊 Tram 4, 9, 14, 20
- ♿ Very good
- 💷 Free
- ↔ Museum Willet-Holthuysen (► 44)

Top: working on diamonds

45

Museum het Rembrandthuis

HIGHLIGHTS

- *Self-portrait with a Surprised Expression*
- *Five Studies of the Head of Saskia and One of an Older Woman*
- *View of Amsterdam*
- *Christ Shown to the People*

INFORMATION

- ➕ J7; Locator map D3
- ✉ Jodenbreestraat 4
- ☎ 5200400; www.rembrandthuis.nl
- 🕐 Mon–Sat 10–5; Sun, public hols 1–5. Closed 1 Jan
- 🚇 Nieuwmarkt, Waterlooplein
- 🚋 Tram 9, 14, 20
- 🚢 Museumboat stop 5
- ♿ Few
- 💲 Expensive
- ❓ Brief film of Rembrandt's life

Below: Self-portrait with Saskia *Rembrandt, 1636*

The absence of Rembrandt's own belongings from this intimate house is more than compensated for by its collection of his etchings, which is virtually complete. They are fascinating.

From riches to rags In this red-shuttered canal house, Rembrandt spent the happiest and most successful years of his life, producing many of his most famous paintings and prints here. Because of his wife, the wealthy heiress Saskia van Uylenburg, the up-and-coming young artist had been introduced to Amsterdam's patrician class and commissions for portraits had poured in. He had rapidly become an esteemed painter, and bought this large, three-storey house in 1639 as a symbol of his newfound respectability. After Saskia's tragic death, age 30, in 1642 shortly after the birth of their son Titus, Rembrandt's work became unfashionable, and in 1656 he was declared bankrupt. The house and most of his possessions were sold in 1658, although Rembrandt continued to live here until 1660. He died a pauper in 1669 (➤ 32). The house is furnished with period fittings, while most of Rembrandt's works are in a separate wing.

Funny faces It is a strange experience to see 260 of the 280 etchings ascribed to Rembrandt in the very surroundings in which they were created. His achievements in etching were as important as those in his painting, since his mastery in this medium inspired its recognition as an art form for the first time. Four of his copper etching plates are also on display, together with a series of biblical illustrations. Look out for Rembrandt's studies of street figures hung alongside some highly entertaining self-portraits in various guises, and some mirror-images of himself making faces.

Magere Brug

This traditional double-leaf Dutch drawbridge is a city landmark, and one of the most photographed sights in Amsterdam at night, illuminated by strings of enchanting lights.

Skinny sisters Of Amsterdam's 1,200 or so bridges, the wooden 'Skinny Bridge' is, without doubt, the best known. Situated on the Amstel river, it is a 20th-century replica of a 17th-century drawbridge. Tradition has it that, in 1670, a simple footbridge was built by two elderly sisters named *Mager* (meaning skinny), who lived on one side of the Amstel and wanted easy access to their carriage and horses, stabled on the other bank. It seems more likely, however, that the bridge took its name from its narrow girth. In 1772 it was widened and became a double drawbridge, enabling ships of heavy tonnage to sail up the Amstel from the IJ, an inlet of what was then a sea called the Zuider Zee and is today the IJsselmeer, a freshwater lake.

City uproar In 1929 the city council started discussing whether to demolish the old frame, which had rotted. It was to be replaced with an electrically operated bridge. After a huge outcry, the people of Amsterdam voted overwhelmingly to save the original wooden bridge.

Speedy opening The present bridge, made of African azobe wood, was erected in 1969 and its mechanical drive installed in 1994. Every now and then, you can watch the bridge master raising the bridge to let boats through. He then jumps on his bicycle and rides hastily upstream to open the Amstel and Hoge sluice gates, only to mount his bike again, return downstream, and repeat the whole procedure.

DID YOU KNOW?

- Around 63,000 boats pass under the bridge each year
- Rebuilding in 1969 cost f140,000
- There are 60 drawbridges in Amsterdam; 8 are wooden

INFORMATION

- J9; Locator map D3
- At Kerkstraat on the Amstel River
- Waterlooplein
- Tram 4, 9, 14, 20
- Museumboat stop 5
- Museum Willet-Holthuysen (► 44), Joods Historisch Museum (► 48)

Top: the Magere Brug, all lit up at night

47

Joods Historisch Museum

HIGHLIGHTS

- Grote Schul (Great Synagogue, 1671)
- Holy Ark (1791)
- Haggadah Manuscript (1734)

DID YOU KNOW?

- 1597 First Jew gained Dutch citizenship
- 1602 Judaism first practised openly here
- 1671 The Grote Schul became the first synagogue in Western Europe
- 102,000 of the 140,000-strong Dutch Jewish community were exterminated in World War II
- Restoration of the synagogues cost over f13 million

INFORMATION

- K8; Locator map D3
- Jonas Daniël Meijerplein 2–4
- 6269945; www.jhn.nl
- Daily 11–5. Closed Yom Kippur
- Café
- Waterlooplein
- Tram 9, 14, 20
- Museumboat stop 5
- Very good
- Moderate

Top: the Great Synagogue

A remarkable exhibition devoted to Judaism and the story of Jewish settlement in Amsterdam. The most memorable and poignant part portrays the horrors of the Holocaust.

Reconstruction Located in the heart of what used to be a Jewish neighbourhood, this massive complex of four former synagogues forms the largest and most important Jewish museum outside Israel. The buildings lay in ruins for many years after World War II, but have since been painstakingly reconstructed as a monument to the strength of the Jewish faith and to the suffering of the Jewish people under the Nazis.

Historical exhibits The New Synagogue (1752) gives a lengthy, detailed history of Zionism, with displays of religious artefacts. The Great Synagogue (1671), of more general interest, defines the role of the Jewish community in Amsterdam's trade and industry. Downstairs is a chilling exhibition from the war years and a moving collection by Jewish painters, including a poignant series entitled *Life? or Theatre?* (1940–42) by Charlotte Salomon, who died in Auschwitz aged 26.

The Dockworker The Nazis occupied Amsterdam in May 1940 and immediately began to persecute the Jewish population. In February 1941, 400 Jews were gathered outside the Great Synagogue by the SS, herded into trucks and taken away. This triggered the February Strike, a general strike led by dockers. Though suppressed after only two days, it was Amsterdam's first open revolt against Nazism and gave impetus to the resistance movement. Every 25 February, a ceremony at Andriessen's statue *The Dockworker* commemorates the strike.

Nederlands Scheepvaart Museum

Holland's glorious seafaring history gets due recognition at this museum, which displays with contemporary flair a fine collection of ships, full-size replicas and models and artefacts.

Admiralty storehouse The vast neoclassical building (1656) that now houses the Maritime Museum was formerly the Dutch Admiralty's central store. Here the East India Company would load their ships prior to the eight-month journey to Jakarta, headquarters of the VOC in Indonesia. In 1973, the arsenal was converted into this museum, which has the largest collection of ships in the world.

Voyages of discovery An ancient dugout, a re-created section of a destroyer, schooners and luxury liners depict Holland's remarkable maritime history. Children can peer through periscopes and operate a radar set, while parents marvel at some 500 magnificent model ships and study the charts, instruments, weapons, maps and globes from the great age of exploration. Don't miss the first-ever sea atlas, the mid-16th century three-masted ship model, or the beautiful royal sloop – the 'golden coach on water' – last used in 1962 for Queen Juliana's silver wedding anniversary.

The *Amsterdam* The highlight of the museum is moored alongside – the *Amsterdam*, a replica of the 18th-century Dutch East Indiaman that sank off the English coast in 1749 during her maiden voyage. A vivid film *Voyage to the East Indies* is shown, and in summer, actors become bawdy 'sailors', firing cannons, swabbing the decks, loading cargo and enacting burials at sea. The *Stad Amsterdam*, a replica of a clipper from 1854, began construction at the wharf in 1999.

HIGHLIGHTS

- The *Amsterdam*
- Royal sloop
- Blaeu's World Atlas (Room 1)
- First printed map of Amsterdam (Room 1)
- Three-masted ship (Room 2)
- Wartime exhibits (Rooms 21–24)

INFORMATION

- M6; Locator map E2
- Kattenburgerplein 1
- 5232222
- Tue–Sun 10–5. Also Mon 10–5 mid-Jun to mid-Sep. Closed 1 Jan, 30 Apr. Crew on board *Amsterdam* in summer Mon–Sat 10:30–4:15; Sun 12:30–4:15. Winter Tue–Sun 11–3
- Restaurant
- Bus 22, 32
- Museumboat stop 6
- Very good
- Expensive
- Artis Zoo (➤ 61), Hortus Botanicus (➤ 60)
- Souvenir and bookshop, model-boat kit shop Thu and Fri only, multimedia theatre. Special exhibition for children, Treasure Island, runs until 5 Jan, 2003

Top: the ornate stern of the replica of the Amsterdam

49

Tropenmuseum

HIGHLIGHTS

- Bombay slums
- Arabian souk
- Bangladeshi village
- Indonesian farmhouse
- Indonesian gamelan orchestra
- Pacific carved wooden boats
- Papua New Guinean Bisj Poles
- Puppet and musical instrument collections

INFORMATION

- ✚ P10; Locator map F3
- ✉ Linnaeusstraat 2
- ☎ 5688215. Children's Museum ☎ 5688233; www.kit.nl/tropenmusem
- 🕐 Mon–Sun 10–5. Closed 1 Jan, 30 Apr, 5 May, 25 Dec. Children's Museum 🕐 Wed afternoons, Sat, Sun; and Mon–Fri during school hols
- 🍴 Ekeko restaurant
- 🚊 Tram 9, 14, 20
- ♿ Very good
- 💷 Expensive
- ↔ Artis Zoo (➤ 61), Hortus Botanicus (➤ 60)
- ❓ Soeterijn Theater. Shop ☎ 5688233 for further information

Top: statue of a Hindu goddess in the Tropenmuseum

In the extraordinary Tropical Museum, once a hymn to colonialism, colourful reconstructions of street scenes with sounds, photographs and slide presentations evoke contemporary life in tropical regions.

Foundations In 1859, Frederik Willem van Eeden, a member of the Dutch Society for the Promotion of Industry, was asked to establish a collection of objects from the Dutch colonies 'for the instruction and amusement of the Dutch people'. The collection started with a simple bow, arrows and quiver from Borneo and a lacquer water scoop from Palembang, then expanded at a staggering rate, as did the number of visitors. In the 1920s, to house the collection, the palatial Colonial Institute was constructed and adorned with stone friezes to reflect Holland's imperial achievements. In the 1970s, the emphasis shifted away from the glories of colonialism towards an explanation of Third World problems. Beside the museum is the Oosterpark, a pleasant green space.

Another world The precious collections are not displayed in glass cases, but instead are set out in lifelike settings, amid evocative sounds, photographs and slide presentations, so that you feel as if you've stepped into other continents. Explore a Bombay slum, feel the fabrics in an Arabian souk, have a rest in a Nigerian bar, contemplate in a Hindu temple or listen to the sounds of Latin America in a café. There is also a theatre, the Soeterijn, where visiting performers mount performances of non-Western music, theatre and dance in the evenings. During the day, activities in the children's section, Kindermuseum TMJunior, give youngsters (aged 6–12) an insight into other cultures.

AMSTERDAM's
best

Canals & Waterways

SUNKEN BOOTY

The canals receive many of the city's unwanted items. More than 100 million litres of sludge and rubbish are removed annually by a fleet of ten municipal boats: six for recovering floating refuse, one for retrieving bikes (about 10,000 a year), using hooks, and three dredgers. Among the so-called treasures they find are stolen wallets, parking meters, cars with failed hand brakes and even an occasional corpse.

AMSTEL
The river is a busy commercial thoroughfare, with barges carrying goods to and from the port. Its sturdy 18th-century wooden sluice gates are closed four times a week. This enables fresh water from the IJmeer to flow into the canal network.
✚ H8–J10   🚋 Tram 4, 9, 14, 16, 20

AMSTERDAM–RHINE CANAL
Amsterdam's longest waterway stretches from the IJ to Switzerland.
✚ Off map   🚌 Bus 37, 220, 245

BLAUWBURGWAL
Amsterdam's shortest canal extends between Singel and Herengracht.
✚ F4   🚋 Tram 1, 2, 5, 13, 17, 20

BLOEMGRACHT AND EGELANTIERSGRACHT
These intimate, narrow thoroughfares in the Jordaan, a retreat from the hustle and bustle of downtown, are lined with colourful small boats.
✚ C4–D5   🚋 Tram 13, 14, 17, 20

BROUWERSGRACHT
Also in the Jordaan, the Brouwersgracht owes its name to the many breweries established here in the 16th and 17th centuries. Houseboats and the old warehouses that line it (once used to store barley but today converted into luxury apartments) make this leafy canal particularly photogenic.
✚ D1–F3   🚉 Centraal Station

The junction of the Keizersgracht and the Reguliersgracht

GROENBURGWAL

This idyllic, picturesque canal near the Muziektheater was Monet's favourite.
🞣 H7   🚇 Nieuwmarkt

THE IJ

Amsterdam is situated on precariously low-lying ground at the confluence of the IJ (an inlet of the IJsselmeer lake) and the Amstel river. During Amsterdam's heyday in the 17th century, most maritime activity was centred on the IJ inlet and along Prins Hendrikkade, where the old warehouses were crammed with spices and other exotic produce from the East. Since 1876, access to the sea has been via the North Sea Canal, and the working docks are now to the west. The IJ is busy with barges sailing to and from the port, with pleasure boats, an occasional warship and cruise liner and the free shuttle ferries to Amsterdam Noord.
🞣 J3   🚇 Centraal Station

A bridge over the Keizersgracht

KEIZERSGRACHT

Together with Prinsengracht and Herengracht, this broad, elegant canal, built in 1612 and named Emperor's Canal after Emperor Maximilian I, completes the Grachtengordel (Canal Ring) – the trio of concentric central canals, that, intersected by a series of narrower, radial waterways, make a cobweb of water across the city. You can skate on it in winter.
🞣 F3–J9   🚋 Tram 1, 2, 5, 13, 14, 16, 17, 20, 24, 25

LEIDSEGRACHT

One of the most exclusive addresses in town.
🞣 D8–E8   🚋 Tram 1, 2, 5, 7, 10, 20

LOOIERSGRACHT

In the 17th century, the main industry in the Jordaan was tanning, hence the name Tanner's Canal. Many streets are named after the animals whose pelts were used such as Hazenstraat (Hare Street), Reestraat (Deer Street) and Wolvenstraat (Wolf Street).
🞣 D7   🚋 Tram 7, 10, 20

OUDEZIJDS ACHTERBURGWAL AND OUDEZIJDS VOORBURGWAL

In contrast to most of Amsterdam's canals, which are peaceful and romantic, parts of the Oudezijds Achterburgwal and Oudezijds Voorburgwal are lined with glaring, neon-lit bars and sex shops.
🞣 H5–H6   🚋 Tram 4, 9, 16, 20, 24, 25

REGULIERSGRACHT

Seven bridges cross the water here in quick succession. They are best viewed from the water at night, when they are lit by strings of lights.
🞣 G9–G10   🚋 Tram 4, 16, 20, 24, 25

OLD DOCKLANDS

Amsterdam ranks among the world's 15 busiest ports, handling 45 million tonnes per year. It is Nissan's European distribution centre and the world's largest cocoa port. The city's old harbour has been taken by developers, but for a taste of its former glory, head for the Scheepvaart Museum (➤ 49) in the Eastern Islands, or to the Western Islands, where the carefully restored 17th-century warehouses, cluttered wharfs and nautical street names like Zeilmakerstraat (Sailmaker Street) and Touwslagerstraat (Rope Factory Street) offer a glimpse of old Amsterdam. (🞣 G3–H3 ✉ north of the railway between Wester-Kanal and Westerdoksdijk).

Districts

In the Top 25
16 ROSSE BUURT (➤ 41)

A typically ornate gable

CHINATOWN

Amsterdam's 7,000-strong Chinese community earns part of its living from the numerous Chinese restaurants around Nieuwmarkt.

➕ J6 🚇 Nieuwmarkt

JODENHOEK

Jewish refugees first came here in the 16th century and settled on the cheap, marshy land southeast of Nieuwmarkt and bordered by the Amstel. Almost the entire district was razed to the ground at the end of World War II, leaving only a few synagogues (➤ 48) and diamond factories as legacy of a once-thriving community.

➕ J7 🚇 Waterlooplein

DE JORDAAN

This popular bohemian quarter with its labyrinth of picturesque canals, narrow streets, trendy shops, cafés and restaurants was once a boggy meadow alongside Prinsengracht. A slum in the 17th century, it later became a more respectable working-class district. The name is believed to have come from the French *jardin*, meaning garden.

➕ D4 🚊 Tram 3, 10, 13, 14, 17, 20

DE PIJP

This lively, multicultural area was once one of Amsterdam's most attractive working-class districts outside the Grachtengordel. The bustling Albert Cuypmarkt takes place daily (➤ 55), and there are several diamond-cutting workshops.

➕ Off F11 🚊 Tram 4, 16, 20, 24, 25

PLANTAGE

The Plantation became one of Amsterdam's first suburbs in 1848. Before that, this popular and leafy residential area was parkland.

➕ M8–N8 🚊 Tram 9, 14, 20

ZEEDIJK

Once the sea wall of the early maritime settlement and until recently the haunt of sailors and shady characters, this area on the fringe of the Red Light District is home to several good bars and restaurants.

➕ H4–J4 🚇 Centraal Station 🚊 Tram 1, 2, 4, 5, 9, 13, 16, 17, 20, 24, 25

GRACHTENGORDEL (CANAL RING)

The buildings along the web of canals around the medieval city centre are supported on thousands of wooden piles to stop them from sinking. Constructed as part of a massive 17th-century expansion project, the immaculate patrician mansions along Prinsengracht, Keizersgracht and Herengracht look almost like a toy town in a child's picture book, with their trim brickwork and characterful gables. The best way to enjoy their architectural details is from the water.

Markets

In the Top 25

🔟 **BLOEMENMARKT (➤ 40)**

ALBERT CUYPMARKT

Amsterdam's biggest, best-known and least expensive general market, named after a Dutch landscape artist, attracts some 20,000 bargain hunters on busy days.

➕ Off F11 ✉ Albert Cuypstraat 🕐 Mon–Sat 10–5 🚋 Tram 4, 16, 20, 24, 25

NOORDERMARKT

For a taste of the Jordaan district, head for the lively square surrounding the Noorderkerk. On Monday morning visit the Lapjesmarkt textile and second-hand clothing market, and on Saturday try the Boerenmarkt for organically grown fresh produce, crafts and birds.

➕ E3 ✉ Noorderstraat 🕐 Mon–Fri 7:30–1; Sat 10–3 🚌 Bus 18, 22, 44; tram 3, 10

OUDEMANHUISPOORT

Antiquarian bookshops in an 18th-century arcade.

➕ G7 ✉ Oudemanhuispoort 🕐 Mon–Fri 11–4 🚋 Tram 4, 9, 16, 20, 24, 25

POSTZEGELMARKT

A specialist market for stamps, coins and medals.

➕ F6 ✉ 280 Nieuwezijds Voorburgwal 🕐 Wed, Sat 1–4 🚋 Tram 1, 2, 5, 20

ROMMELMARKT

Rommel means rummaging. Bric-a-brac is your cue to the style of the place.

➕ D7 ✉ Looiersgracht 38 🕐 Daily 11–5 🚋 Tram 7, 10, 17, 20

WATERLOOPLEIN FLEA MARKET

Amsterdam's liveliest market, full of funky clothes, curiosities and 'antique' junk.

➕ J7 ✉ Waterlooplein 🕐 Mon–Sat 9–5 🚇 Waterlooplein

ZWARTE MARKT

This huge indoor flea market outside Amsterdam (reputedly Europe's largest) has an Eastern Market overflowing with oriental merchandise.

➕ Off map to northwest ✉ Industriegebied aan de Buitenlandenden, Beverwijk-Oost 🕐 Sat 7–5; Sun (Eastern Market only) 8–6 🚉 Beverwijk-Oost

---

MARKETS

Amsterdam resembles a collection of villages, each having its own local market. The daily markets at Ten Katestraat (Kinkerstraat) (➕ F5–F6) and Dapperstraat (➕ K6) are good for fruit and vegetables, and there is a flower market at Amstelveld (➕ H6) every Monday morning. Sunday art markets are held at Spui from March until Christmas (➕ G5–H5) and at Thorbeckeplein from mid-March until November (➕ H6), while you may find a bargain at the Nieuwmarkt antiques market (➕ H5) on Sundays in summer.

Albert Cuypmarkt

55

Bridges, Buildings & Monuments

BRIDGES

No other city in the world has so many bridges: 1,281. The majority are single or triple-arched hump-backed bridges made of brick and stone with simple cast-iron railings. The oldest bridge is the Torensluis (1648) and the best example of a traditional Dutch drawbridge is the Magere Brug (Skinny Bridge ► 47). The cast-iron Blauwbrug (Blue Bridge, 1874) is one of the most traditional, while the 20th-century Waals Eilandsgracht bridge, with its geometric arches, is the most modern.

BEURS VAN BERLAGE

Designed by Hendrik Berlage and now hailed as an early modernist masterpiece, the former stock exchange provoked outrage when it opened in 1903. It is now a concert hall (► 80).

✚ G5　✉ Damrak 243　☎ 5304113　🕐 Tue–Sun 11–5 for exhibitions　🚊 Tram 4, 9, 16, 20, 24, 25

CENTRAAL STATION

Many travellers get their first glimpse of Amsterdam's architectural wonders at P J H. Cuyper's vast neoclassical station (1889), standing defiantly with its back to the River IJ.

✚ J3　✉ Stationsplein　☎ 5578400　🚉 Centraal Station

CONCERTGEBOUW

The orchestra and main concert hall of this elaborate neoclassical building have been renowned worldwide ever since the inaugural concert in 1888.

✚ Off C11　✉ Concertgebouwplein 2–6　☎ 6718345　🕐 Box office daily 10–7　🚊 Tram 3, 5, 12, 16, 20

99 Rokin, a modern interpretation of a canalside house

ENTREPOTDOK

The old warehouses at Entrepotdok have been converted into offices and expensive apartments.

✚ N8　✉ Entrepotdok　🚌 Bus 22

GREENPEACE HEADQUARTERS

This pragmatic city seems an appropriate home for the Greenpeace world headquarters, in a remarkable *Jugendstil* (art nouveau) building dating from 1905.

✚ E4　✉ Keizersgracht 174　☎ 4223344　🚊 Tram 13, 14, 17, 20

KERWIN DUINMEYER MONUMENT

Kerwin, a 15-year-old black youth, was stabbed to death in Amsterdam in 1983. It was the first time since World War II that someone had been killed in the city because of race. His statue stands in the Vondelpark as a symbol of the Dutch fight against racism.

✚ Off map　✉ Vondelpark (Jacob Obrechtstraat exit)　🚊 Tram 2, 3, 5, 12, 20

'T LIEVERDJE

In the 1960s this little bronze statue of a boy, which

stands so innocently in the middle of the square,
became a symbol of the *Provo* movement, and
rallying point of frequent anti-establishment
demonstrations. The name means Little Darling.
➕ F7 ✉ Spui
🚊 Tram 1, 2, 5, 20

MUNTTOREN
The tower of the
former Mint was part
of the southern
gateway to the
medieval city.
➕ G8 ✉ Muntplein
🚊 Tram 4, 9, 14, 16, 20,
24, 25

MUZIEKTHEATER
Amsterdam's theatre
for opera and dance is
known locally as the
false teeth because of
its white marble
panelling and red
brick roof. The
complex includes the
uninspiring buildings
of the new town hall
(Stadhuis). The
design caused great
controversy when it
was built in 1986,
sparking riots during
its construction.
➕ J8 ✉ Waterlooplein
22 🚇 Waterlooplein

*National Monument in
Dam square, in memory
of World War II victims*

NATIONAL MONUMENT
The 23-m obelisk in Dam square contains soil from
all the Dutch provinces and former colonies. Every
year on 4 May, the Queen lays a wreath here.
➕ G5 ✉ Dam 🚊 Tram 4, 9, 14, 16, 20, 24, 25

SCHEEPVAARTHUIS
The peculiarly tapered Maritime House, encrusted
with marine decoration, suggests the bow of an
approaching ship. Commissioned by seven shipping
companies in 1912, it represents one of the most
impressive examples of the architecture of the
Amsterdam School.
➕ J5 ✉ Prins Hendrikkade 108–111 🚌 Bus 22, 32

SCHREIERSTOREN
The Weeping Tower was where tearful wives and
girlfriends waved farewell to their seafaring menfolk.
They had good reason to weep: in the 18th century,
voyages took up to four years and many sailors died.
➕ J4 ✉ Prins Hendrikkade 94–95 🚇 Centraal Station

HOMOMONUMENT
One of the city's more
arresting sculptures is the
Homomonument (1987) by
Dutch artist Karin Daan, on
the corner of Westermarkt and
Keizersgracht. Consisting of
three pink, granite triangles,
the sign homosexuals were
forced to wear during the
German Occupation, it
commemorates all those who
have been persecuted because
of their homosexuality.

57

Museums & Galleries

CANAL-HOUSE MUSEUMS

The grand 17th-century canal house Museum van Loon (Keizersgracht 672) has an impressive family portrait gallery. The Theatermuseum (Herengracht 168) and the Bijbels Museum (Bible Museum) (Herengracht 366), with its religious artefacts, are also in beautiful houses whose interiors alone warrant a visit.

A mug of Heineken

MUSEUM PASSES

If you intend to visit several museums and galleries, buy a *Museumjaarkaart* from the VVV (tourist office) for 31.80 euros/f70 for adults, 13.60 euros/f30 up to 24 years. It will give you free entry into over 400 museums throughout Holland for one year. The *Amsterdam Pass* also offers various discounts, and only costs 29 euros/f63.95.

In the Top 25

🎟 **AMSTERDAMS HISTORISCH MUSEUM (► 37)**
🎟 **ANNE FRANKHUIS (► 33)**
🎟 **FILM MUSEUM (VONDELPARK) (► 26)**
🎟 **HASH MARIHUANA HEMP MUSEUM (► 41)**
🎟 **JOODS HISTORISCH MUSEUM (► 48)**
🎟 **MUSEUM AMSTELKRING (► 43)**
🎟 **MUSEUM HET REMBRANDTHUIS (► 46)**
🎟 **MUSEUM WILLET-HOLTHUYSEN (► 44)**
🎟 **NEDERLANDS SCHEEPVAART MUSEUM (► 49)**
🎟 **RIJKSMUSEUM (► 30)**
🎟 **VAN GOGH MUSEUM (► 28)**
🎟 **STEDELIJK MUSEUM (► 27)**
🎟 **TROPENMUSEUM (► 50)**

HEINEKEN EXPERIENCE

Free tastings of the world's best-known brand of Dutch beer are offered after a look at an interactive celebration of Heineken's first brewery.
➕ F11 ✉ Stadhouderskade 78 ☎ 5239666/5239436
🕐 Tue–Sun 10–6. Last admissions at 5 🚊 Tram 4, 6, 7, 10, 16, 24, 25
♿ Few (phone in advance) 🍴 Moderate ❓ No under 18s

MUSEUM AVIODOME

The National Aerospace Museum has aircraft from 1903 to the '1990s, in addition to models of early balloons and heavier-than-air aircraft.
➕ Off A1 ✉ Westelijke Randweg 201, Schiphol-Centrum ☎ 4068000
🕐 Apr–Sep: 10–5. Oct–Mar: Tue–Fri 10–5; Sat, Sun 12–5. Closed 1 Jan, 25 and 31 Dec 🚉 Schiphol ♿ Good 🍴 Expensive

VERZETSMUSEUM (RESISTANCE MUSEUM)

Rare wartime memorabilia and a fascinating summary of the Dutch resistance during World War II.
➕ L7 ✉ Plantagekerklaan 61a ☎ 6202535 🕐 Tue–Fri 10–5; Sat, Sun, Mon 12–5. Closed 1 Jan, 30 Apr, 25 Dec 🚊 Tram 7, 9, 14, 20 ♿ Good 🍴 Moderate

WERF 'T KROMHOUT MUSEUM

Located at one of the city's few remaining working shipyards, this 18th-century factory building documents the development of Eastern Islands shipbuilding industry.
➕ P7 ✉ Hoogte Kadijk 147 ☎ 6276777 🕐 Tue 10–4
🚌 Bus 22, 28 ♿ Few 🍴 Inexpensive

WOONBOOTMUSEUM (HOUSEBOAT MUSEUM)

If you've ever wondered what life is like aboard one of Amsterdam's 2,500 houseboats, here's your chance to find out. The *Hendrika Maria*, built in 1914, was a working canal barge before being converted.
➕ D5 ✉ By Prinsengracht 296 ☎ 4270750 🕐 Wed–Sun 11–5
Nov–Feb: Fri–Sun 11–5 🚊 Tram 1, 2, 5 ♿ None 🍴 Inexpensive

Places of Worship

AMSTELKERK
Squat and wooden, this Calvinist church (1670) was originally meant to be a temporary structure while funds were raised for a larger building elsewhere.
➕ H10 ✉ Amstelveld ☎ 6238138 🕓 Closed to public except during 10:30AM Sun service 🚊 Tram 4

FRANCISCUS XAVERIUSKERK
This splendid neo-Gothic church is often dubbed De Krijtberg (Chalk Hill), because it is built on the site of a former chalk merchant's house.
➕ F7 ✉ Singel 442–448 ☎ 6231923 🕓 Services only 🚊 Tram 1, 2, 5, 20

NOORDERKERK
An austere church, the first in Amsterdam to be constructed in the shape of a Greek cross. It was built in 1620–23 for the Protestant workers in the Jordaan district, and is still well attended.
➕ E3 ✉ Noordermarkt 44–48 ☎ 6266436 🕓 Sat 11–1; Mon 10:30–1 and services 🚊 Tram 3, 10, 13, 14, 17, 20

PORTUGUESE SYNAGOGUE
Holland's finest synagogue, one of the first of any size in Western Europe. It is remarkable that this imposing building escaped destruction in World War II.
➕ K8 ✉ Mr Visserplein 3 ☎ 6245351 🕓 Sun–Fri 10–4, and service on Sat at 9AM. Closed Jewish holidays, Sun 10–noon 🚇 Waterlooplein ⛴ Museumboat stop 5 🎫 Inexpensive

SINT NICOLAASKERK
Amsterdam's main Roman Catholic church (1888) and one of many Dutch churches named after St Nicholas, the patron saint of sailors. St Nicholas is also *Sinterklaas* (see panel).
➕ J4 ✉ Prins Hendrikkade 73 ☎ 6248749 🕓 Mon–Sat 11–4, and services 🚊 Tram 1, 2, 4, 5, 9, 13, 16, 17, 20, 24, 25

ZUIDERKERK
Holland's first Protestant church (1614) and indisputably one of the city's most beautiful. Its designer, Hendrick de Keyser, lies buried within. The distinctive 80-m high tower affords spectacular views of the Nieuwmarkt district.
➕ H6 ✉ Zuiderkerkhof 72 ☎ 6892565 🕓 Mon–Wed, Fri 12–5; Thu 12–8 🚇 Nieuwmarkt

Zuiderkerk

SINTERKLAAS

St Nicholas, or *Sinterklaas*, pays an early visit to the city each year on the third Saturday of November. Accompanied by *Zwarte Piet* (Black Peter), he arrives by boat near Sint Nicolaaskerk and distributes gingerbread to children, then receives the keys to the city from the mayor on Dam square. On 5 December (*Sinterklaasavond or Pakjesavond*) he comes during the night with sacks of presents for the sleeping children.

59

Parks & Gardens

In the Top 25

🟦 **OOSTERPARK, TROPENMUSEUM (➤ 50)**
🟦 **VONDELPARK (➤ 26)**

HORTUS BOTANICUS

Laid out in 1682, the botanical gardens were originally sponsored by the Verenigde Oost-Indishche Compagnie (VOC) whose members brought back plants and seeds from all corners of the earth, to be grown and studied by doctors and apothecaries here. One such plant , a coffee tree given to Louis XIV of France and cultivated in his American colonies, was the ancestor of the Brazilian coffee plantations. Likewise, the production of palm oil in Indonesia is due to plants initially cultivated here.

AMSTELPARK

A formal rose garden and a rhododendron valley are two of the seasonal spectacles at this magnificent park, created in 1972 for an international horticultural exhibition. It also offers pony rides, miniature golf, a children's farm, the Rieker windmill (➤ 62) and other attractions. There is a special walk for blind people, and in summer you can tour the park in a miniature train.

➕ Off Q9 ⏰ Dawn–dusk 🍴 Restaurant and café 🚌 Bus 69, 148, 169

AMSTERDAMSE BOS

Amsterdam's largest park was built on the polders in the 1930s as part of a job creation scheme. It is a favourite family destination on weekends whatever the season. In winter, there is tobogganing and skating, in summer swimming, sailing and biking. A leisurely tram ride can be taken through the park in colourful antique cars acquired from various European cities.

➕ Off map ✉ Anstelveen ⏰ Always open 🍴 Open-air pancake restaurant and café 🚌 Bus 170, 171, 172

HORTUS BOTANICUS

With more than 8,000 plant species, Amsterdam's oldest botanical garden (1638) boasts one of the largest collections in the world. It has spectacular tropical greenhouses, a medicinal herb garden orchid nursery and a monumental cycad that, at 400 years old, is reputed to be the world's oldest potted plant.

➕ K8 ✉ Plantage Middenlaan 2a ☎ 6258411 ⏰ Apr–Sep: Mon–Fri 9–5; Sat, Sun 11–5. Oct–Mar: Mon–Fri 9–4; Sat, Sun 11–4 🍴 Café 🚊 Tram 7, 9, 13, 20 ♿ Good 💰 Moderate

SARPHATIPARK

Enjoy a picnic bought at nearby Albert Cuypmarkt (➤ 55) in this tiny green oasis dedicated to the 19th-century Jewish doctor and city benefactor, Samuel Sarphati.

➕ Off G11 ⏰ 9–dusk 🚊 Tram 3, 4, 16, 20, 24, 25

Vondelpark

For Children

ARTIS ZOO (NATURA ARTIS MAGISTRA)

As well as animals, the complex includes museums, an aquarium and the Planetarium (hourly shows).
🔢 M9 ✉ Plantage Kerklaan 38–40 ☎ 5233400; www.artis.nl
🕐 Tue–Sun 9–5; Mon 12:30–5 🍴 Restaurant and café 🚊 Tram 7, 9, 14, 20. Artis Express boat from Centraal Station 🚹 Good
✋ Expensive

CIRCUS ELLEBOOG

Learn tightrope walking, juggling and other circus skills at the Elleboog Circus. You need to book.
🔢 D8 ✉ Passeerdersgracht 32 ☎ 6269370 🕐 Times vary, phone for details 🚊 Tram 7, 10, 20 🚹 Good ✋ Expensive

DE KRAKELING THEATER

Mime and puppet shows, for under-12s, and over-12s.
🔢 C8 ✉ Nieuwe Passeerderstraat 1 ☎ 6253284 🕐 Shows Thu–Sat 8PM; Sun, Wed 2PM 🚊 Tram 7, 10, 20 🚹 Good
✋ Moderate

KINDERKOOKKAFÉ

A children's restaurant where children between five and twelve can cook, then serve or eat at mini-tables.
🔢 G6 ✉ Oudeijds Achterburgwal 193 ☎ 6253257 🕐 Sat cooking 3:30–6, dinner 6–8 (age 8 plus). Sun cooking 2:30–5, high tea 5–6 (age 5 plus). Mon–Fri 1–3 🚇 Nieuwmarkt ✋ Expensive

KINDERBOERDERIJ DE PIJP

A farm especially for children at the heart of the city.
🔢 Off F11 ✉ Lizzy Ansinghstraat 82 ☎ 6648303 🕐 Mon–Fri 11–5; Sat, Sun 1–5 🚊 Tram 24, 25 🚹 Few ✋ Free

MADAME TUSSAUD SCENERAMA

Wax models of Rembrandt, Pavarotti, Schwarzenegger and other characters from the 17th century to the present day, and an amazing 5-m giant clothed in windmills and tulips.
🔢 G6 ✉ Dam 20 ☎ 52221010 🕐 Sep–Jun: 10–5:30. Mid-Jul to Aug: 9:30–7:30. Closed 30 Apr 🚊 Tram 4, 9, 14, 16, 20, 24, 25 🚹 Good ✋ Very expensive

NEMO (NEWMETROPOLIS)

Children will enjoy learning at this impressive hands-on, interactive museum of modern technology.
🔢 L5 ✉ Oosterdok 2 ☎ 0900 9191100 🕐 Tue–Sun 10–5. Open daily during school holidays 10–5. Closed 1 Jan, 30 Apr, 25 Dec 🍴 Café 🚌 Bus 22, 32 🚹 Very good ✋ Expensive

OUT OF TOWN

Ask the VVV for details on making excursions to Volendam, where villagers still wear traditional costume, the windmill village of Zaanse Schans, to Zuiderzee, for the reconstructed fishing village of Enkhuizen, or to one of Holland's many theme parks, such as the enchanted forest of De Efteling at Kaatsheuvel or the Duinrell water park at Wassenaar, near The Hague.

PUNCH & JUDY

From mid-April until the end of September there are free Punch and Judy performances on Wed 1–5 in Dam square.

Owl statue at the zoo

Windmills

Amsterdam's most central windmill has been converted into a bar

D'ADMIRAAL
Built in 1792 to grind chalk but now unused.
🏠 Off map ✉ Noordhollandsch Kanaaldijk, near Jan Thoméepad
🚌 Bus 34, 37, 39, 242

DE BLOEM
This old grain mill, built in 1768, resembles a giant pepper shaker.
🏠 Off map ✉ Haarlemmerweg, near Nieuwpoortkade 🚌 Bus 18

DE GOOIER (FUNENMOLEN)
Amsterdam's most central mill (1725) was the first grain mill in Holland to use the streamlined sails that became ubiquitous. Built on a brick base, with an octagonal body and a thatched wooden frame, it has been converted into a small brewery and bar (► 83), but its massive sails still occasionally creak into action.
🏠 Q8 ✉ Funenkade 🚋 Tram 6, 10; bus 22

DE RIEKER
The finest windmill in Amsterdam was built in 1636 to drain the Rieker polder, and is situated at the southern tip of the Amstelpark. This was one of Rembrandt's favourite painting locations – there is a small statue near by in his memory. The windmill has been beautifully preserved and is now a private home.
🏠 Off map ✉ Amsteldijk, near De Borcht 🚌 Bus 148

NATIONAL WINDMILL DAY

Windmills have been a feature of the Dutch landscape since the 13th century. Much of the Netherlands lies below sea level, and windmills were used to drain the land and extend the shoreline, creating the fertile farmland called *polder*. Some 950 survive, and on National Windmill Day (the second Saturday in May), many turn their sails and are open to the public.

1100 ROE
This old smock mill, shaped like a peasant's smock, was one of a '*gang*' of water mills that once drained the polders. It stands 1,100 roes from the city's outer canal. The word *roe* means both the flat part of a sail that had to be set or reefed according to wind strength, and a unit of measurement (about 28cm) used to calculate the distance from the city centre.
🏠 Off map ✉ Herman Bonpad, Sportpark Ookmeer 🚌 Bus 19, 23

1200 ROE
This early 17th-century post mill, with its impressive platform and revolving cap, was built to help drain the polders.
🏠 Off map ✉ Haarlemmerweg, near Willem Molengraaffstraat
🚌 Bus 85

AMSTERDAM
where to...

Dutch Restaurants

OPENING TIMES AND PRICES

The restaurants listed on pages 64–71 are all open for lunch and dinner daily unless otherwise stated. They are divided into three price categories. For a main dish, expect to pay:

£££ over 27 euros/f60
££ up to 27 euros/f60
£ up to 13.50 euros/f30

DUTCH TREATS

Numerous restaurants in the city provide a taste of authentic Dutch cuisine. The most delicious dishes include thick split-pea soup (*erwtensoep*), meaty stews (*stamppot*), smoked eel (*gerookt paling*), raw herring (*haring*), sweet and savoury pancakes (*pannekoeken*), waffles (*stroopwafels*) and cheeses. Look out for the special 'Neerlands Dis' sign (a red, white and blue soup tureen), which indicates restaurants commended by this organisation for their top-quality traditional Dutch cuisine.

A recent trend is towards 'New Dutch' cuisine. Traditional dishes are prepared with a lighter touch and presented with greater sophistication, using fresh seasonal products and an adventurous mix of herbs and spices.

DE BLAUWE HOLLANDER (£)

Generous portions of wholesome and modestly priced fare in a lively bistro setting.

✚ E9 ✉ Leidsekruisstraat 28, Grachtengordel ☎ 6233014 🕐 Dinner only 🚊 Tram 1, 2, 5, 6, 7, 10, 20

DORRIUS (£££)

A sophisticated take on rustic Dutch style. Try the pike and salted cod traditional delicacies, or the cheese soufflé.

✚ G4 ✉ Crowne Plaza Hotel, Nieuwezijds Voorburgwal 5, Centrum ☎ 4202224 🚊 Tram 1, 2, 5, 13, 17, 20

DE GROENE LANTAARN (££)

This tiny restaurant, located on a quiet leafy canal, specialises in Gouda fondues.

✚ C5 ✉ Bloemgracht, Jordaan ☎ 620088 🚊 Tram 10, 13, 14, 17

HAESJE CLAES (££)

Dutch cuisine at its best, served in a warren of small, panelled dining rooms in this building in Centrum dating from the 16th-century.

✚ F7 ✉ Spoistraat 275, Centrum ☎ 6249998 🚊 Tram 1, 2, 5

DE KEUKEN VAN 1870 (£)

Originally a soup kitchen, this old-fashioned establishment serves huge platefuls of no-frills food at communal tables.

✚ G4 ✉ Spuistraat 4, Centrum ☎ 6248965 🕐 Mon–Fri 12:30–8; Sat, Sun 4–9 🚊 Tram 1, 2, 5, 13, 17, 20

MOLEN DE DIKKERT (£££)

Dine in a majestic old windmill on the outskirts of Amsterdam.

✚ Off map to south ✉ Amsterdamseweg 104 ☎ 6411378 🕐 Closed Sat–Mon for lunch 🚌 Bus 160

DE POORT (££)

Since 1870, this famous restaurant has sold nearly 6 million numbered steaks. Every thousandth one comes with a free bottle of house wine.

✚ F5 ✉ Hotel Die Port van Cleve, Nieuwezijds Voorburgwal 176, Centrum ✉ 6240047 🚊 Tram 1, 2, 5, 13, 17, 20

DE ROODE LEEUW (££)

The brasserie-style Red Lion serves up good stews and sauerkraut dishes.

✚ G5 ✉ Amsterdam Hotel, Damrak 93–94, Centrum ☎ 5550666 🕐 10AM–11PM, last orders 9:30PM 🚊 Tram 4, 9, 16, 20, 24, 25

'T SWARTE SCHAEP (££)

The Black Sheep is noted for its rustic atmosphere, excellent wines, and varied classic and modern cuisine.

✚ D9 ✉ Korte Leidsedwarsstraat 24, Grachtengordel ☎ 6223021 🚊 Tram 1, 2, 5, 6, 7, 10, 20

D'VIJFF VLIEGHEN (£££)

The menu in the Five Flies in five 17th-century houses has an impressive collection of 'New Dutch' dishes.

✚ F7 ✉ Spuistraat 294–302, Centrum ☎ 6248369 🕐 Dinner only 🚊 Tram 1, 2, 5

Elegant Dining

DE BELHAMEL (££)

Art nouveau and classical music set the tone for polished Continental cuisine in an intimate, often crowded setting with a superb canal view.
✚ G3 ✉ Brouwersgracht 60, Jordaan ☎ 6221095
🕐 Dinner only 🚌 Bus 18, 22

BORDEWIJK (£££)

Mediterranean and Asian touches, and a spare, black-and-white interior, add zest to French dishes.
✚ E3 ✉ Noordermarkt 7, Jordaan ☎ 6243899
🕐 Dinner only. Closed Mon 🚌 Bus 18, 22

CAFÉ ROUX (££)

Fine French cuisine in an art nouveau setting, overlooked by a Karl Appel mural.
✚ H5 ✉ Grand Hotel, Oudezijds Voorburgwal 197, Centrum ☎ 5553560
🚇 Nieuwmarkt

CHRISTOPHE (£££)

Chef Jean-Christophe Royer combines French style and US experience to great effect in his chic canalside restaurant.
✚ E4 ✉ Leliegracht 46, Jordaan ☎ 6250807
🕐 Dinner only. Closed Sun 🚊 Tram 13, 14, 17, 20

LE CIEL BLEU (£££)

The height of stylish French cuisine on the Okura Hotel's 23rd floor.
✚ Off F11 ✉ Ferdinand Bolstraat 333, De Pijp ☎ 6787111 🕐 Dinner and Sun brunch 🚊 Tram 12, 25

LE GARAGE (£££)

French regional cuisine at its best at this trendy brasserie in a converted garage near Vondelpark.
✚ Off E11 ✉ Ruysdaelstraat 54–56, Oud Zuid ☎ 6797176
🕐 Dinner daily, lunch Mon–Fri.
🚊 Tram 3, 5, 12, 20

DE GOUDEN REAL (£££)

French restaurant in a 17th-century dockside building with a romantic waterside terrace.
✚ Off F1 ✉ Zandhoek 14, Westerdok ☎ 6233883
🕐 Closed Sun 🚊 Tram 3; bus 35

LA RIVE (£££)

In Amsterdam's most expensive hotel. Robert Kraneborg may have left but present chef Edwin Katz produces excellent regional French cooking.
✚ Off map ✉ Roelof Hartstraat 6–8, Oud Zuid ☎ 6765201 🕐 Closed Sat, Sun, and lunch Mon 🚊 Tram 3, 12, 20, 24

DE SILVEREN SPIEGEL (£££)

An exquisite classic menu, complemented by one of the city's best wine lists, in a superbly restored 1614 house. Fish is a speciality.
✚ G3 ✉ Kattengatt 4–6, Centrum ☎ 6246589
🕐 Dinner only. Closed Sun except for reserved parties
🚊 Tram 1, 2, 5, 13, 17, 20

HET TUYNHUIS (££)

Sophisticated French, Portuguese and Dutch cuisine in a converted coach house and garden.
✚ F8 ✉ Reguliersdwars-straat 28, Grachtengordel ☎ 6276603 🕐 Closed Sat and Sun lunch 🚊 Tram 4, 9, 14, 16, 20, 24, 25

TIPPING

Most restaurant windows display menus giving the price of individual dishes including BTW (tax) and a 15 per cent service charge. Nevertheless, most Amsterdammers leave a small tip or round up the bill. This tip should be left as change rather than included on a credit-card payment.

Indonesian Restaurants

A HEARTY MEAL

When the Dutch took over the Spice Islands of the East Indies in the 17th century, they got more than spices out of their new colony. They developed a taste for the exotic local cuisine that survived Indonesian independence and gives Amsterdam today an abundance of *Indonesisch* restaurants.

First-timers to an Indonesian restaurant should order a *rijsttafel*, which includes rice and a complete range of other dishes: *ayam* (chicken), *ikam* (fish), *telor* (egg), *rendang* (beef), *krupuk* (shrimp crackers), shredded coconut and sweet-and-sour vegetables. The *rijsttafel* ('rice table') originally referred to the long list of ingredients required to prepare such a feast. It originated in early colonial days among hungry Dutch planters who, not satisfied by the basic Indonesian meal of rice and vegetables accompanied by meat or fish, continually added other dishes. Thus the rijsttafel was born, a meal that ranges from a 6- to 10-item mini-rijsttafel to a 20- to 30-dish feast.

ANEKA RASA (££)

This airy modern restaurant offers numerous vegetarian dishes including an all-vegetarian *rijsttafel*.
➕ H4 ✉ Warmoesstraat 25–29, Centrum ☎ 6261560 🕐 Dinner only 🚋 Centraal Station

BOJO (££)

Popular late-night eatery serving huge portions of rice and noodle dishes and delicious satays. Good size portions, and plenty of vegetarian choices too.
➕ D9 ✉ Lange Leidsedwarsstraat 51, Grachtengordel ☎ 6249706 🕐 Dinner Mon–Fri; Sat, Sun lunch, dinner 🚋 Tram 1, 2, 5

INDRAPURA (££)

A popular colonial-style restaurant. Tell the waiter how hot and spicy you want your dishes to be.
➕ G8 ✉ Rembrandtplein 40-42, Grachtengordel ☎ 6237329 🕐 Dinner only 🚋 Tram 4, 9, 14, 20

KANTJIL EN DE TIJGER (££)

Modern décor and spicy, imaginative Javanese cuisine. Try the delicious *Masi Rames*, a mini-*rijsttafel* on one plate.
➕ F7 ✉ Spuistraat 291, Centrum ☎ 6200994 🕐 Dinner only 🚋 Tram 1, 2, 5

ORIENT (££)

This dark, opulent restaurant specialises in *rijsttafels*, with more than 20 different sorts, three of them vegetarian, and an extensive buffet on Wednesdays. A good introduction to Indonesian flavours.
➕ C11 ✉ Van Baerlestraat 21, Oud Zuid ☎ 6734958 🕐 Dinner only 🚋 Tram 2, 3, 5, 12, 20

SAHID JAYA (££)

Shady courtyard garden, especially nice in summer.
➕ F8 ✉ Reguliersdwarsstraat, Grachtengordel 26 ☎ 6263727 🚋 Tram 16, 24, 25

SAMA SEBO (££)

Rush mats and batik typify this Balinese setting where you can select from the menu to create your own *rijsttafel*.
➕ D8 ✉ P C Hooftstraat 27, Oud Zuid ☎ 6628146 🕐 Closed Sun 🚋 Tram 2, 3, 5, 12, 20

SARANG MAS (££)

Modern surroundings counterpoint traditional cuisine.
➕ G4 ✉ Damrak 44, Centrum ☎ 6222105 🕐 Daily 11.30AM–11PM 🚋 Tram 4, 9, 16, 20, 24, 25

SUKASARI (£)

Colourful batik tablecloths, closely packed tables, generous portions.
➕ G6 ✉ Damstraat 26-28, Centrum ☎ 6240092 🕐 Dinner Tue–Sat; Mon lunch 🚋 Tram 4, 9, 16, 20, 24, 25

TEMPO DOELOE (££)

One of Amsterdam's best Indonesian restaurants, notable for its western interior, exotic flowers and some of the hottest dishes in town. Booking essential.
➕ H9 ✉ Utrechtsestraat 75, Grachtengordel ☎ 6256718 🕐 Dinner only 🚋 Tram 4

Fish & Vegetarian Restaurants

BODEGA KEYSER (££)
An Amsterdam institution next door to the Concertgebouw, specialising in fish and Dutch dishes.
✚ Off C11 ✉ Van Baerlestraat 96, Oud Zuid ☎ 6711441 ⏰ Mon–Sat 9AM–midnight; Sun 11AM–midnight 🚊 Tram 2, 3, 5, 12, 20

DE OESTERBAR (££)
The seasonal delights of this elegant fish restaurant include herring in May, mussels in June and delicate Zeeland oysters throughout the summer.
✚ D9 ✉ Leidseplein 10, Grachtengordel ☎ 6232988 ⏰ Daily 12–midnight 🚊 Tram 1, 2, 5, 6, 7, 10, 20

LE PECHEUR (£££)
A smart fish-bistro with a secluded garden. Outstanding fresh oysters, caviar, sashimi and lobster.
✚ F8 ✉ Reguliersdwarsstraat 32, Grachtengordel ☎ 6243121 ⏰ Closed Sat lunch and all day Sun 🚊 Tram 1, 2, 5

PIER 10 (£££)
Former shipping office with an innovative menu that emphasises fish.
✚ H2 ✉ De Ruijterkade, Pier 10, Centrum ☎ 6248276 ⏰ Dinner only 🚊 Tram 1, 2, 4, 5, 9, 13, 16, 17, 20, 24, 25 🚉 Centraal Station

VIS AAN DE SCHELDE (££)
This popular fish restaurant boasts an eclectic menu of fish dishes from around the world. Dine in art deco interior or outside on patio.
✚ Off F11 ✉ Scheldeplein 4, De Pijp ☎ 6248276 ⏰ Dinner only 🚌 Bus 15, 245

VISRESTAURANT JULIA (£)
Julia's famous fish platter, with ten kinds of fish, baked, barbecued and grilled, draws people from all over the region.
✚ Off map to south ✉ Amstelveenseweg 160 ☎ 6/95394 ⏰ Dinner only. Closed Mon 🚌 Bus 146, 147, 170, 171, 172

VEGETARIAN

DE BOLHOED (£)
A trendy restaurant on the edge of the Jordaan, with vegetarian pâtés, salads and hearty vegan dishes.
✚ E3 ✉ Prinsengracht 60-62, Grachtengordel ☎ 6261803 🚊 Tram 13, 14, 17, 20

GOLDEN TEMPLE (£)
An imaginative menu of Indian, Mexican and Middle Eastern dishes.
✚ H9 ✉ Utrechtsestraat 126, Grachtengordel ☎ 6268560 ⏰ Dinner only 🚊 Tram 4

HEMELSE MODDER (££)
Sophisticated main courses and delicious desserts including 'Heavenly Mud', the chocolate mousse from which the restaurant takes its name.
✚ J5 ✉ Oude Waal 9, Centrum ☎ 6243203 ⏰ Dinner only 6–10 (last admission). Closed Mon 🚇 Nieuwmarkt

FISH AND VEGETABLES
Although the Dutch eat a lot of meat, Amsterdam with its sea-going associations has a great choice of fish restaurants. Vegetarians, too, have speciality eating places to suit all tastes and budgets, while others, most notably pizzerias and the Asian restaurants around town, offer vegetarian menu-dishes.

International Fare

SURINAMESE CUISINE

Explore the narrow streets of the multiracial district around Albert Cuypstraat, and you will soon realise how easy it is to eat your way around the world in Amsterdam. The many Surinamese restaurants here serve a delicious blend of African, Chinese and Indian cuisine. Specialties include *bojo* (cassava and coconut quiche) and *pitjil* (baked vegetables with peanut sauce). Try them at Marowijne (✉ Albert Cuypstraat 68–70), or Wan Pipel (✉ Albert Cuypstraat 140).

ASIAN CARIBBEAN EXPERIENCE (£)
More than 100 dishes from all over Asia and the Caribbean.
⊞ G5 ✉ Warmoesstraat 170, Centrum ☎ 6271545
⏱ Dinner only ◻ Tram 4, 9, 16, 20, 24, 25

DE BRAKKE GROND (£–££)
Flemish Cultural Centre's darkly atmospheric restaurant, serving bountiful portions of Belgian food. There is a great choice of Belgian beers to complement your meal.
⊞ G6 ✉ Nes 43, Centrum ☎ 6260044 ⏱ Tue–Sat noon–1AM; Sun, Mon 12–7
◻ Tram 4, 9, 14, 16, 20, 24, 25

CAFÉ PACIFICO (£)
The most authentic Mexican bodega in town. Especially crowded on Tuesday, which is *margarita* night.
⊞ H4 ✉ Warmoesstraat 31, Centrum ☎ 6242911
⏱ Centraal Station

CHEZ GEORGES (££)
Fine Belgian cuisine in a classical, candlelit setting.
⊞ F4 ✉ Herenstraat 3, Grachtengordel ☎ 6263332
⏱ Closed Sun, Wed ◻ Tram 1, 2, 5, 13, 17, 20

DYNASTY (£££)
A sophisticated, sumptuously decorated garden restaurant with fine Southeast Asian cuisine.
⊞ F8 ✉ Reguliersdwarsstraat 30, Grachtengordel
☎ 6268400 ⏱ Dinner only. Closed Tue ◻ Tram 16, 24, 25

EL RANCHO ARGENTINIAN GRILL (££)
Sizzling steaks and spare ribs in a wood-panelled, jolly-gaucho setting that brings a taste of the pampas to Amsterdam.
⊞ F7 ✉ Spui 3, Centrum ☎ 6256764
⏱ 11AM–midnight ◻ Tram 4, 9, 14, 16, 20, 24, 25

DE FLES BISTRO (££)
Cosy cellar, full of large wooden tables. A real locals' hangout.
⊞ G9 ✉ Corner of Prinsengracht and Vijzelstraat 137, Grachtengordel
☎ 6249644 ⏱ Dinner only ◻ Tram 16, 24, 25

FROMAGERIE CRIGNON CULINAIR (£)
Rustic restaurant with eight different types of cheese fondue.
⊞ F5 ✉ Gravenstraat 28, Centrum ☎ 6246428
⏱ Tue–Sat dinner only ◻ Tram 4, 9, 16, 20, 24, 25

MEMORIES OF INDIA (£££)
Tandoori, Moghlai and vegetarian cuisine in a refined colonial setting.
⊞ G8
✉ Reguliersdwarsstraat, Grachtengordel 88 ☎ 6235710
⏱ Dinner only ◻ Tram 16, 24, 25

PAKISTAN (££)
Holland's top Pakistani restaurant. The menu ranges from traditional, village dishes to highly spiced specialities.
⊞ Off F11 ✉ Scheldestraat 100, De Pijp ☎ 6753976
⏱ Dinner only ◻ Tram 12, 25

PASTA E BASTA (££)

Pasta in chic surroundings, with opera classics.
🟦 F9 ✉ Nieuwe Speigelstraat 8, Grachtengordel ☎ 4222229 🕐 Dinner only 🚋 Tram 16, 24, 25

ROSE'S CANTINA (££)

Excellent value Tex Mex meals in lively, sociable surroundings. Probably Amsterdam's most crowded restaurant.
🟦 F8 ✉ Reguliersdwarsstraat 38-40, Grachtengordel ☎ 6259797 🕐 Dinner only 🚋 Tram 16, 24, 25

RUM RUNNERS (££)

Giant palms, caged parrots, live music, spicy stews and cocktails feel distinctly tropical.
🟦 D5 ✉ Prinsengracht 277, Grachtengordel ☎ 6274079 🕐 Mon–Sat from 4PM; Sun from 2PM 🚋 Tram 13, 14, 17, 20

SAUDADE (££)

A Portuguese restaurant with dockside terrace, at the heart of the fashion-able Entrepotdok district.
🟦 M8 ✉ Entrepotdok 36, Oost and Oosterdok ☎ 6254845 🕐 Dinner only. Closed Tue 🚌 Bus 22

SEA PALACE (££)

Advertised as Europe's first floating restaurant, the Sea Palace is modelled on a Chinese pagoda-style palace.
🟦 K4 ✉ Oosterdokskade 8, Oost & Oosterdok ☎ 6264777 🚌 Bus 22

SHERPA (£)

Nepalese/Tibetan restaurant with traditional Himalayan ornaments.
🟦 F8 ✉ Korte

Leidsedwarsstraat 58, Grachtengordel ☎ 6239495 🕐 Dinner only (and lunch in summer) 🚋 Tram 1, 2, 5, 6, 7, 10, 20

SHIBLI (£££)

Sit on a sofa inside a Bedouin tent, dining on an Arabian banquet.
🟦 G5 ✉ Hotel Krasnapolsky, Dam 9, Centrum ☎ 4723291 🕐 Wed–Sat dinner only 🚋 Tram 4, 9, 16, 20, 24, 25

TANGO (££)

Small, candlelit and on the edge of the Red Light District. Try the huge, juicy steaks.
🟦 H5 ✉ Warmoesstraat 49, Centrum ☎ 6272467 🕐 Dinner only 🚋 Tram 4, 9, 16, 20, 24, 25

TEPPANYAKI NIPPON (££)

One of Holland's most exclusive Japanese grill-restaurants.
🟦 F8 ✉ Reguliersdwarsstraat 18–20, Grachtengordel ☎ 620878/ 🕐 Dinner only 🚋 Tram 16, 24, 25

TOSCANINI (££)

The best Italian food in town. Book well ahead.
🟦 D3 ✉ Lindengracht 75, Jordaan ☎ 6232813 🕐 Dinner only. Closed Sun 🚋 Tram 3

LE ZINC... ET LES DAMES (££)

Home-style French cuisine in a converted canalside warehouse. The *tarte tatin* is superb.
🟦 G10 ✉ Prinsengracht 999, Grachtengordel ☎ 6229044 🕐 Dinner only. Closed Sun, Mon 🚋 Tram 4

DUTCH SUSHI

Long before Japanese sushi became fashionable fast food in Europe, the Low Countries already had their own version – raw herring – accompanied by chopped onion and pickles. Be sure to try some at one of the herring stalls dotted around town. Kromhout (at the junction of Singel and Raadhuisstraat), and Volendammer Viswinkel (le van der Helststraat 60) are considered two of the best.

Snacks & *Eetcafés*

A BITE TO "EET"

Try an *eetcafé* for filling homemade fare – soup, sandwiches and omelettes. Remember that kitchens close around 9PM. Browse market stalls for local delicacies. Most bars offer *borrelhapjes* (mouthfuls with a glass) – usually olives, chunks of cheese or *borrelnoten* (nuts with a savoury coating). More substantial *borrelhapjes* are *bitterballen* (bitter balls), fried balls of vegetable paste; and *vlamaetjes* (little flames), spicy mini spring rolls. For a really quick snack, the many Febo company's food dispensers about town are cheap: simply put your money in and your snack comes out hot.

CAFÉ DANTZIG (£)

Giant, crusty baguettes with delicious fillings for a lunch on the terrace beside the Amstel river.
➕ H7 ✉ Zwanenburgwal 15, Centrum ☎ 6209039
🕐 10AM–1AM (Fri, Sat until 2AM)
Ⓠ Waterlooplein

CAFÉ MOKO (££)

A delightfully located café-cum-restaurant on the corner of Prinsengracht and Reguliersgracht, with a charming shady terrace beside the canals.
➕ H9 ✉ Amstelveld 12, Grachtengordel ☎ 6261199
🕐 Closed Tue 🚊 Tram 4

GARY'S MUFFINS (£)

Fresh filled bagels, muffins and brownies.
➕ D6 ✉ Prinsengracht 454, Grachtengordel ☎ 4201452
🕐 Mon–Fri 9–5:30; Sat, Sun 9–6 🚊 Tram 1, 2, 5, 13, 17, 20

KAAS-WIJNHUIS (£)

A charming delicatessen-cum-*eetcafé* with wines, cheeses, cold cuts, pâtés.
➕ G5 ✉ Warmoesstraat 16, Centrum ☎ 6230878
🕐 Mon–Sat 10–6. Closed Sun
Ⓠ Centraal Station

LUNCHROOM DIALOGUE (£)

A warehouse cellar, away from the crowds at Anne Frankhuis next door; good for sandwiches and cakes.
➕ D5 ✉ Prinsengracht 261a, Grachtengordel ☎ 6239991
🕐 Mon–Sat 9:30–5; Sun 10–5
🚊 Tram 13, 14, 17, 20

MORITA-YA (£)

Traditional Japanese snackbar with floor seating as well as tables, that's a must for sushi fans.
➕ J4 ✉ Zeedijk 18, Centrum
☎ 6380756 🕐 Dinner only.
Closed Wed Ⓠ Centraal Station

PANCAKE BAKERY (£)

The best pancakes in town.
➕ E4 ✉ Prinsengracht 191, Grachtengordel ☎ 6251333
🚊 Tram 13, 14, 17, 20

LA PLACE (£)

A self-service 'indoor market' restaurant. Choose your dish at one of the stands, watch it being cooked, then eat at one of the tables.
➕ G7 ✉ Rokin 164, Centrum
☎ 6202364 🕐 10–8 except Thu 10:30–9; Sun, Mon 11–8
🚊 Tram 4, 9, 14, 16, 20, 24, 25

SMALL TALK (££)

Near the Museumplein, this *eetcafé* is ideal for soups and snacks between gallery visits.
➕ C11 ✉ Van Baerlestraat 52, Oud Zuid ☎ 6714864
🕐 Mon–Sat 10–9:30; Sun 10–8:30 🚊 Tram 2, 3, 5, 12, 20

TAPAS CATALÀ (£)

Enjoy a quick bite or a meal of tempting Catalan tapas dishes.
➕ F7 ✉ Spuistraat 299, Centrum ☎ 6231141 🕐 Mon, Wed–Fri 4PM–midnight; Sat, Sun 1PM–midnight 🚊 Tram 1, 2, 5

VAN DOBBEN (£)

A renowned sandwich shop. Try the meat croquette roll that Van Dobben himself makes from a 53-year-old recipe.
✉ Korte Reguliersdwarsstraat 5–9, Grachtengordel
☎ 6244200 🕐 Mon–Thu 9:30AM–1AM; Fri–Sat 9:30AM–2AM; Sun 11:30AM–8PM
🚊 Tram 4, 9, 14, 20

Cafés & Tea Shops

CAFÉ AMÉRICAIN (£)

Artists, writers and bohemians frequent this grand art deco café.

✚ D9 ✉ American Hotel, Leidseplein 26, Grachtengordel ☎ 6245322 🕐 7AM–1AM 🚋 Tram 1, 2, 5, 6, 7, 10, 20

CAFÉ ESPRIT (£)

Designer café, all glass and aluminium, run by the clothing chain next door; popular stop for shoppers.

✚ F7 ✉ Spui 10a, Centrum ☎ 6221967 🕐 Mon–Sat 10–6 (Thu until 10PM); Sun noon–6 🚋 Tram 1, 2, 4, 5, 9, 14, 16, 20, 24, 25

CAFÉ VERTIGO (££)

Brown café-style surroundings, where menu-dishes occasionally reflect themes in the Film Museum. Lovely terrace.

✚ B10 ✉ Vondelpark 3, Oud Zuid ☎ 6123021 🚋 Tram 3, 12

GELATERIA JORDINO (£)

Bright and breezy place that does great home-made Italian ice-cream and waistline-threatening chocolate cake.

✚ E1 ✉ Haarlemmerdijk 25, Centrum ☎ 4203225 🕐 Daily 10–8 🚋 Bus 18, 22

GREENWOOD'S (£)

Homely little English-style tearoom serving up scones with jam and cream, chocolate cake and lemon-meringue pie.

✚ F4 ✉ Singel 103, Grachtengordel ☎ 6237071 🕐 Daily 9:30–7 🚋 Tram 1, 2, 5, 13, 17, 20

NIEUWE KAFÉ (£)

The café's crowded terrace on Dam square provides a captive audience for street musicians; ideal for people-watching.

✚ G5 ✉ Eggertstraat 8, Centrum ☎ 6272830 🕐 9–6 🚋 Tram 4, 9, 14, 16, 20, 24, 25

POMPADOUR (£)

The finest chocolatier in town doubles as a sumptuous tearoom.

✚ E7 ✉ Huidenstraat 12, Grachtengordel ☎ 6239554 🕐 Tue–Fri 9:30–5.45; Sat 9–5:30 🚋 Tram 1, 2, 5

LA RUCHE (£)

Treat yourself to coffee with waffles piled high with strawberries and cream in this café in De Bijenkorf department store (► 74), overlooking Dam square.

✚ G5 ✉ 1 Dam, Centrum ☎ 6218080 🕐 Mon 11–6; Tue–Sat 9:30–6; Thu, Fri 9:30–9; Sun noon–6 🚋 Tram 4, 9, 14, 16, 20, 24, 25

WINKEL (£)

A popular café looking out onto the Noordermarkt (► 55). Great for people-watching when the markets are on.

✚ E3 ✉ Noordermarkt 43, Jordaan ☎ 6230223 🕐 Sat, Mon lunch, all day Sun 🚋 Tram 3, 10

COFFEE SHOPS

In Amsterdam, the expression 'coffee shop' refers to the 'smoking' coffee shops, where mostly young people hang out, high on hash. 'Smoking' coffee shops are usually easily recognisable by their psychedelic decor, thick fog of bitter smoke and mellow clientele. The cake on sale is sure to be drug-laced 'space cake'. Surprisingly, many such shops do a good cup of coffee.

71

Shopping Areas

SHOPPING TIPS

Although Amsterdam does not compare with Paris or London for European chic, the large number of unusual specialist shops, second-hand shops and colourful markets among its more than 10,000 shops and department stores, make shopping a real pleasure. Interesting souvenirs and gifts to take home are easy to find, whatever your budget.
Most shops are open Tuesday to Saturday from 9AM or 10AM until 6PM, on Mondays from 1PM until 6PM, on Thursdays until 9PM. Many shops open noon–5PM on Sundays, too. Cash is the usual method of payment, although credit cards and Eurocheques are accepted at most department stores and larger shops.

DUTCH GIFTS

Bulbs
Made-to-measure clogs
Bottle of *jenever* (Dutch gin)
Edam or Gouda cheese
Diamonds
Leerdam crystal
Makkum pottery
An old print or map of the city
Delftware – if you want the real thing look for De Porcelyne Fles in Delft itself
(► 21).

ART & ANTIQUES

Antique shops are concentrated in the *Spiegelkwartier* near the Museumplein, along and by Nieuwe Spiegelstraat and along the Rokin. Countless galleries are scattered throughout the city, although many can be found along the main canals. The De Looier Kunst- & Antiekcentrum on Elandsgracht in the Jordaan brings together dozens of art and antiques dealers in an indoor market. Other places to buy art, though not originals, are museum shops that sell high-quality poster reproductions of the famous artworks on their walls, by both Dutch and international artists. Look for the best of these at the Rijksmuseum, Van Gogh Museum, Stedelijk Museum of Modern Art and Museum het Rembrandthuis.

BOOKSHOPS

Most bookshops, including the American Book Center and a branch of British chain Waterstone's in Kalverstraat, are around the university district (off the Spui) and in Leidsestraat. You will also find several specialist antique bookshops on Nieuwezijds Voorburgwal, and there is an indoor antiquarian book market at Oudemanhuispoort.

FASHION

The three main shopping thoroughfares – Kalverstraat, Nieuwendijk, and Leidsestraat – are lined with international chain stores and mainstream outlets for clothing and accessories. To the south, you'll find designer stores, including Armani, Azorro and Rodier, along P C Hooftstraat, van Baerlestraat and Beethovenstraat. For more adventurous garb, head for the Jordaan.

OFFBEAT SHOPS

Tiny specialist shops and boutiques selling everything from psychedelic mushrooms to designer soap and kitsch toilet furniture can be found all over the city. Many are in the Jordaan and along the web of sidestreets that connect the ring canals between Leidsegracht and Brouwersgracht.

SECOND-HAND

Explore the second-hand shops of the Jordaan for a bargain, or sift through local street markets, including the city's largest and wackiest flea market at Waterlooplein.

SHOPPING MALLS

There are five main shopping malls: chic Magna Plaza near Dam square; De Amsterdamse Poort, reached by metro at Amsterdam Zuidoost; Winkelcentrum Boven 't IJ, reached by ferry across the IJ; Winkelcentrum Amstelveen in the southern suburbs, reached by tram 5; and Schiphol Plaza at the airport, open from 7AM until 10PM daily.

Dutch Souvenirs

AMSTERDAM SMALLEST GALLERY

An original painting of the city bought here will remind you of your stay.

✉ Westermarkt 60
☎ 6223756 🚊 Tram 13, 14, 17, 20

BLUE GOLD FISH

Storehouse of fantastical gifts including jewellery, ornaments, home fixtures and fabrics.

✉ Rozengracht 17
☎ 6233134 🚊 Tram 13, 14, 17, 20

BONEBAKKER

Holland's royal jewellers, with dazzling displays of gold and silverware. Enjoyable even if you can't afford to buy.

✉ Rokin 88–90 ☎ 6232294
🚊 Tram 4, 9, 14, 16, 20, 24, 25

DAM SQUARE SOUVENIRS

Located in Centrum, this souvenir shop has a wide choice of clogs, furnishings, pottery and T-shirts.

✉ Dam 17 ☎ 6203432
🚊 Tram 4, 9, 14, 16, 20, 24, 25

FOCKE & MELTZER

A superior gift shop, with Delft Blue porcelain from De Porcelyne Fles, as well as outstanding Tichelaars Makkumware pottery, Leerdam crystal and locally made silver.

✉ Gelderlandplein 149
☎ 6444429 🚌 Bus 148, 149, 219

HEINEN HANDPAINTED DELFTWARE

Tiny but delightful for its Delftware plates, tulip vases and Christmas decorations.

✉ Prinsengracht 440
☎ 6278299 🚊 Tram 1, 2, 5, 13, 17, 20

HOLLAND GALLERY DE MUNT

Miniature ceramic canal houses, dolls in traditional costume, ornately decorated wooden boxes and trays.

✉ Muntplein 12 ☎ 6232271
🚊 Tram 4, 9, 14, 16, 24, 25

HET KANTENHUIS

Exquisite handmade Dutch lace.

✉ Kalverstraat 124
☎ 6248618 🚊 Tram 4, 9, 14, 16, 20, 24, 25

DE KLOMPENBOER

Authentic clog factory offers the city's largest selection of hand-crafted footwear.

✉ Nieuwezijds Voorburgwal 20
☎ 6230632 🚊 Tram 1, 2, 5, 13, 17, 20

METZ & CO

Expensive gifts and designer furniture. One of the city's most stylish department stores. It has a café on the top floor.

✉ Keizersgracht 455
☎ 5207020 🚊 Tram 1, 2, 5

DE TUIN

The Bloemenmarkt (➤ 40) is the least expensive place to buy bulbs and this stall has the widest selection.

✉ Bloemenmarkt (opposite Singel 502) ☎ 6254571
🚊 Tram 4, 9, 14, 16, 20, 24, 25

TAX-FREE SHOPPING

If you live outside the European Union, you may claim a tax refund of 13.5 per cent on purchases of 136 euros/f300 or more in one shop in one day. At shops bearing the Tax Free Shopping logo, ask for a Global Refund Cheque when you pay. You must export your purchases within 3 months of buying them. At departure to a non-European Union country, go to customs and present your purchases and receipts to have your Global Refund Check validated. You can obtain a cash refund in Schiphol's departure hall, or arrange for a charge-card credit or certified cheque. You should allow around an hour to do this.

If you are travelling by train or car from Holland, you need to go through this procedure at your point of exit from the European Union (if you want to take advantage of the refund scheme). You cannot validate the shopping cheque at Holland's borders with neighbouring countries, because they are EU members.

Food, Drink & Department Stores

SAY CHEESE!

Think Dutch cheese and the distinctive red *Edammer* (from Edam) and *Goudse* (from Gouda) spring to mind. They can be young (*jong*) and mild, or more mature (*belegen*) and strong. Mild young cheeses such as *Leerdammer* and *Maaslander* deserve a tasting, too. Others to try are *Friese Nagelkaas*, flavoured with cumin and cloves and *Gras Kaas* (grass cheese), sold in summer, which owes its especially creamy flavour to the freshness of spring's cow pastures.

DE BIERKONING
850 beers and glasses from around the world.
✉ Paleisstraat 125
☎ 6252336 🚊 Tram 1, 2, 5, 13, 14, 17, 20

DE BIJENKORF
Amsterdam's busy main department store, the *Bijenkorf* (Beehive) lives up to its name.
✉ Dam 1 ☎ 6218080
🚊 Tram 4, 9, 14, 16, 20, 24, 25

EICHHOLTZ
Established delicatessen with Dutch, American, and English specialities.
✉ Leidsestraat 48
☎ 6220305 🚊 Tram 1, 2, 5

GEELS EN CO
Holland's oldest coffee-roasting and tea-trading company, full of heady aromas, with a helpful staff and traditional setting.
✉ Warmoesstraat 67
☎ 6240683 🚊 Tram 4, 9, 14, 16, 20, 24, 25

HENDRIKSE PATISSERIE
Queen Beatrix buys her pastries here.
✉ Overtoom 472 ☎ 6180472
🚊 Tram 1, 6

H P DE VRENG
Celebrated wine-and-spirits establishment, producing fine liqueurs and *jenevers* since 1852.
✉ Nieuwendijk 75
☎ 6244581 🚊 Tram 1, 2, 5, 13, 17, 20

J G BEUNE
Famous for chocolate versions of *Amsterdammertjes* (the posts lining the streets to prevent cars parking on the pavement), and a mouth-watering array of cakes and other bonbons.
✉ Haarlemmerdijk 156
☎ 6248356 🚊 Tram 1, 2, 5, 13, 17, 20

MAISON DE BONNETERIE
A gracious department store, popular with wealthy ladies.
✉ Rokin 140–2/Kalverstraat 183 ☎ 6262162 🚊 Tram 4, 9, 14, 16, 20, 24, 25

VITALS VITAMIN-ADVICE SHOP
Vitamins, minerals and other food supplements, plus a unique service: a computerised vitamin test that proposes vitamin supplements based on your age and lifestyle.
✉ Nieuwe Nieuwstraat 47
☎ 6257298 🚊 Tram 1, 2, 5, 13, 17, 20

VROOM & DREESMAN
Clothing, jewellery, perfumes, electronic and household goods.
✉ Kalverstraat 201-203
☎ 6220171 🚊 Tram 4, 9, 14, 16, 20, 24, 25

DE WATERWINKEL
A hundred different mineral waters.
✉ Roelof Hartstraat 10
☎ 6755932 🚊 Tram 3, 12, 20, 24

WOUT ARXHOEK
One of the best cheese shops, with over 250 different varieties.
✉ Damstraat 19 ☎ 6229118
🚊 Tram 4, 9, 14, 16, 20, 24, 25

Antiques & Books

AMERICAN BOOK CENTER
Four floors of English-language books, plus US and British magazines and newspapers and games.
✉ Kalverstraat 185
☎ 6255537 🚊 Tram 4, 9, 14, 16, 20, 24, 25

AMSTERDAM ANTIQUES GALLERY
Six dealers under one roof, selling silver, pewter, paintings, and Dutch tiles, among other items.
✉ Nieuwe Spiegelstraat 34
☎ 6253371 🚊 Tram 6, 7, 10

ATHENAEUM BOEKHANDEL
This bookshop, in a striking art nouveau building, stocks international newspapers and specialises in social sciences, literature and the classics.
✉ Spui 14–16 ☎ 6226248
🚊 Tram 1, 2, 5

EDUARD KRAMER
Old Dutch tiles, the earliest dating from 1580.
✉ Nieuwe Spiegelstraat 64
☎ 6230832 🚊 Tram 6, 7, 10

EGIDIUS ANTIQUARISCHE BOEKHANDEL
A tiny shop packed with antique books on travel, photography and the arts.
✉ Nieuwezijds Voorburgwal 334
☎ 6243929 🚊 Tram 1, 2, 5

DE KINDER-BOEKWINKEL
Children's books, arranged according to age.
✉ Rozengracht 34
☎ 6224761 🚊 Tram 13, 14, 17, 20

LAMBIEK
The world's oldest comic shop.
✉ Kerkstraat 78 ☎ 6267543
🚊 Tram 1, 2, 5

DE LOOIER KUNST- & ANTIEKCENTRUM
A covered antiques market with hundreds of stalls selling everything from quality items to junk.
✉ Elandsgracht 109
☎ 6249038 🚊 Tram 7, 10, 17, 20

PREMSELA & HAMBURGER
Fine antique jewellery and silver in a refined setting.
✉ Rokin 120 ☎ 6249688
🚊 Tram 4, 9, 14, 16, 20, 24, 25

SCHELTEMA, HOLKEMA EN VERMEULEN
The city's biggest bookshop, with a floor of computer software, and audio and video titles.
✉ Koningsplein 20
☎ 5231411 🚊 Tram 1, 2, 5

DE SLEGTE
Amsterdam's largest second-hand bookshop is good for bargains.
✉ Kalverstraat 48–52
☎ 6225933 🚊 Tram 4, 9, 14, 16, 20, 24, 25

'T CACHOT
Second-hand thrillers and crime novels in the jail of what was once Holland's smallest police station.
✉ Dorpsplein ☎ 6691795
🕐 Tue, Wed, Sat afternoons only
🚌 Bus 59, 60, 175

GOING, GOING, GONE!

Amsterdam's main auction houses are Sotheby's (✉ De Boelelaan 30 ☎ 5502200) and Christie's (✉ Cornelis Schuytstraat 57 ☎ 5755255). Their Dutch counterpart, Veilinghuis (Auction House) de Nieuwe Zon, is at Molukkenstraat 200 (☎ 6168586). All hold presale viewings, interesting even if you have no intention of buying.

Specialist Shops

MAGNA PLAZA

Amsterdam's most luxurious shopping mall, Magna Plaza, is in an imposing neo-Gothic building in Nieuwezijds Voorburgwal near Dam square. Its four floors are filled with upmarket specialist shops, such as Pinokkio, for educational toys; Bjorn Borg, for sporty underwear; and Speeldozenwereld, for quaint musical boxes. There is a café on the top floor and a Virgin Megastore in the basement.

ANIMATION ART

Drawings, paintings and figurines of famous cartoon characters from Superman to Tintin and the Smurfs.
✉ Nieuwendijk 91–93
☎ 6277600 ▣ Tram 1, 2, 4, 5, 9, 13, 16, 17, 20, 24, 25

CENTAUR GALLERY

Finely crafted traditional toys and sculptures by master woodcarver, Bruno Jonker, in a 17th-century dyke-house studio.
✉ Nieuwendijk 14
☎ 6240219 ▣ Tram 1, 2, 5, 13, 17

DE BEESTENWINKEL

A cuddly-toy shop for adults. Ideal for collectors and small gifts.
✉ Staalstraat 11 ☎ 6231805
▣ Tram 4, 9, 14, 16, 20, 24, 25

CHRISTMAS WORLD

Sample the special atmosphere of Christmas in Holland all year round, amid glittering displays of candles and bells.
✉ Nieuwezijds Voorburgwal 137–9 ☎ 6227047 ▣ Tram 1, 2, 5, 13, 17, 20

CONCERTO

Finest all-round selection of new and used records and CDs to suit all tastes. Especially good for jazz, classical music and hits from the 1950s and '60s.
✉ Utrechtsestraat 52–60
☎ 6245467 ▣ Tram 4

CONSCIOUS DREAMS

Anything's possible in Amsterdam. This shop specialises in 'magic mushrooms'!
✉ Kerkstraat 117

☎ 6266907 ▣ Tram 16, 24, 25

DEN HAAN & WAGENMAKERS

A quilt-maker's paradise of traditional fabrics, tools and gadgets.
✉ Nieuwezijds Voorburgwal 97–9 ☎ 6202525 ▣ Tram 1, 2, 5, 13, 17, 20

DE FIETSENMAKER

One of the top bike shops in Amsterdam.
✉ Nieuwe Hoogstraat 21–23
☎ 6246137 Ⓜ Nieuwmarkt

FIFTIES-SIXTIES

A jumble of period pieces including toasters, records, lamps and other mementos of this hip era.
✉ Huidenstraat 13
☎ 6232653 ▣ Tram 1, 2, 5

FROZEN FOUTAIN

Not only is this striking interiors shop a dazzling showcase for up-and-coming Dutch designers, it is a fabulous place for finding unusual gifts, ceramics and jewellery.
✉ Prinsengracht 629 ☎ 622 9375 ▣ Tram 1, 2, 5

HEAD SHOP

The shop for marijuana paraphernalia and memorabilia ever since it opened in the 1960s.
✉ Kloveniersburgwal 39
☎ 6249061 Ⓜ Nieuwmarkt

HEMP WORKS

Designer hemp shop: jeans, jackets, shirts, shampoo and soap all made of hemp.
✉ Nieuwendijk 13
☎ 4211762 ▣ Tram 1, 2, 5, 13, 17, 20

JACOB HOOIJ
Old-fashioned apothecary, selling herbs, spices and homeopathic remedies since 1743.
✉ Kloveniersburgwal 12
☎ 6243041 🚇 Nieuwmarkt

KITSCH KITCHEN
Ghanaian metal furniture, Indian bead curtains, Mexican tablecloths, Chinese pots and pans – the whole world in one colourful kitchen!
✉ 1e Bloemdwarsstraat 21
☎ 62228261 🚊 Tram 13, 14, 17, 20

LE SAVONNEREA
A veritable *pot pourri* of bathtime products and accessories. You can even have your own personal text inscribed on the delicious handmade soaps.
✉ Prinsengracht 294
☎ 4281139 🚊 Tram 4, 13, 17, 20

OTTEN & ZOON
Some Dutch people still clomp around in wooden *klompen* (clogs). This shop makes fine wearable ones as well as souvenirs.
✉ Eerste Van der Helstraat 31
☎ 6629724 🚊 Tram 16, 24, 25

OUTRAS COISAS
Ancient and modern pots and gardening tools, reflecting the Dutch passion for plants.
✉ Herenstraat 31 ☎ 6257281
🚊 Tram 1, 2, 5, 13, 17, 20

PARTY HOUSE
A cornucopia of paper decorations, dressing-up clothes, masks and practical jokes.
✉ Rozengracht 93a–b
☎ 6247851 🚊 Tram 13, 14, 17, 20

PAS-DESTOEL
Furniture and interiors designed with a touch of innocent fantasy for children.
✉ Westerstraat 260
☎ 4207542 🚊 Tram 3, 10

P G C HAJENIUS
One of the world's finest tobacco shops, in elegant, art deco premises.
✉ Rokin 92–96 ☎ 6237494
🚊 Tram 4, 9, 14, 16, 20, 24, 25

SCALE TRAIN HOUSE
Take home a do-it-yourself windmill or canal barge kit as a souvenir, or choose from the vast stock of model railway components.
✉ Bilderdijkstraat 94
☎ 6122670 🚊 Tram 3, 12, 13, 14

DE SPEELMUIS
A splendid collection of handmade wooden toys and doll's house miniatures.
✉ Elandsgracht 58
☎ 6385342 🚊 Tram 7, 10, 17, 20

WORLD OF WONDERS
Interior design shop with upmarket fabrics and furnishings, and many small items to enliven your living space.
✉ P C Hooftstraat 129
☎ 4707332 🚊 Tram 2, 3, 5, 12, 20

OIBIBIO
This department store-cum-spiritual centre (✉ Prins Hendrikkade 20–21) offers environmentally friendly clothing (in cotton, wool and hemp), natural cosmetics and gifts, (including some made from recycled glass, paper and leather). The store includes a bookstore, a café and an entire floor dedicated to workshops and therapy treatments, including yoga, tai chi and shiatsu. You can even learn to play the didgeridoo here.

Fashion

BARGAINS

There are often excellent bargains to be found in Amsterdam, especially during the January and July sales. Watch for signs saying *Uitverkoop* (closing-down or end-of-season sale), *Solden* (sale) and *Korting* (discounted goods).

ANALIK

Simple, elegant designs are the hallmark of this boutique belonging to Anakujm, Amsterdam's foremost young designer.
✉ Hartenstraat 36
☎ 4220561 🚋 Tram 1, 2, 5, 13, 14, 17, 20

CORA KEMPERMAN

Elegant and imaginative, fashionable yet Bohemian, individually designed women's fashion.
✉ Leidsestraat 72
☎ 6251284 🚋 Tram 1, 2, 5

ESPRIT

Young, trendy designs for the seriously fashionable.
✉ Spui 10a ☎ 6221967
🚋 Tram 1, 2, 5

HESTER VAN EEGHEN

Handbags, wallets and other leather accessories in innovative shapes, styles and colours, designed in Holland and made in Italy.
✉ Hartenstraat 1 ☎ 6269212
🚋 Tram 13, 14, 17, 20

DE KNOPENWINKEL

The Button Shop boasts over 8,000 different kinds of buttons from all over the world.
✉ Wolvenstraat 14
☎ 6240479 🚋 Tram 1, 2, 5

THE MADHATTER

Handmade hats by Dutch designers.
✉ Van der Helstplein 4
☎ 6647748 🚋 Tram 3, 12, 25

MEXX

Top designer boutique where you'll find many leading French and Italian labels.

✉ P C Hooftstraat 118
☎ 6750171 🚋 Tram 2, 3, 5, 12, 20

OGER

One of the top menswear boutiques.
✉ P C Hooftstraat 81
☎ 6768695 🚋 Tram 2, 3, 5, 12, 20

OILILY

Children love the brightly coloured and patterned sporty clothes of this Dutch company.
✉ P C Hooftstraat 131–133
☎ 6723361 🚋 Tram 2, 3, 5, 12, 20

OSCAR

Outrageous footwear from glittery platforms to psychedelic thigh boots.
✉ Nieuwendijk 208–10
☎ 6253143 🚋 Tram 4, 9, 14, 16, 20, 24, 25

PALETTE

The smallest shop in the Netherlands has a large selection of silk and satin shoes, in 500 colours.
✉ Nieuwezijds Voorburgwal 125
☎ 6393207 🚋 Tram 4, 9, 14, 16, 20, 24, 25

RETRO

Way-out fashion, including a dazzling array of 1960s and '70s flower-power clothing.
✉ Ze Constantijn Huygenstraat 57 ☎ 6834180 🚋 Tram 1, 3, 6, 12

SISSY-BOY

A Dutch clothing chain with stylish, affordable clothing for men and women.
✉ Leidsestraat 15
☎ 6238949 🚋 Tram 1, 2, 5

Theatre, Dance & Cinema

THEATRE & DANCE

FELIX MERITIS
An important avant-garde
dance and drama centre,
and home to the Felix
Meritis experimental
theatre company.
✉ Keizersgracht 324
☎ 6262321 🚊 Tram 13, 14,
17, 20

DE KLEINE KOMEDIE
The very best cabaret and
stand-up comedy, in one
of the city's oldest
theatres.
✉ Amstel 56 ☎ 6240534
🚊 Tram 4, 9,
14, 20

KONINKLIJK THEATER CARRÉ
The Royal Theatre hosts
long-running international
musicals, revues, cabaret,
folk dancing and an
annual Christmas circus.
✉ Amstel 115–25
☎ 6225225 🚊 Weesperplein

MUZIEKTHEATER
An Amsterdam cultural
mainstay and home to the
Nederlands Opera and the
Nationale Ballet since it
opened in 1986, Holland's
largest auditorium, seating
1,689, mounts an
international repertoire as
well as experimental
works. Guided backstage
tours on Wed and Sat at
3PM (➤ 57).
✉ Waterlooplein 22
☎ 6255455 (recorded
information in Dutch; hold for
operator) 🚊 Waterlooplein

STADSSCHOUWBURG
Classical and modern plays
form the main repertoire of
the stylish, 19th-century
Municipal Theatre.

✉ Leidseplein 26 ☎ 6242311
🚊 Tram 1, 2, 5, 6, 7, 10, 20

DE STALHOUDERIJ
One of the city's very few
English-language theatre
companies, in a converted
stable that seats 40.
✉ 1e Bloemdwarsstraat 57
☎ 6264088 🚊 Tram 13, 14,
17, 20

VONDELPARK OPENLUCHTTHEATER
The open-air theatre in
the park offers free drama,
cabaret, concerts and
children's programmes
from June to August.
✉ Vondelpark 🚊 Tram 1, 2,
3, 5, 6, 12, 20

FILMS

CITY 1–7
Amsterdam's largest
multiscreen cinema.
✉ Kleine Gartmanplantsoen 15
☎ 0900 1458 🚊 Tram 1, 2, 5,
6, 7, 10, 20

FILM MUSEUM CINEMATHEEK
International programmes,
ranging from silent films
to more recent releases.
✉ Vondelpark 3 ☎ 5891400
🚊 Tram 1, 2, 3, 5, 6, 12, 20

TUCHINSKI THEATER
Holland's most attractive
and prestigious cinema,
with six screens; the
classic art deco interior
alone makes it worth
visiting, no matter what's
showing.
✉ Reguliersbreestraat 26–28
☎ 6262633
🚊 Tram 4, 9, 14, 20

FILM GUIDE

The city's main multiscreen
cinema complexes, in the
Leidseplein and
Rembrandtplein areas, follow
Hollywood's lead closely. The
latest big US releases and
British films that become
international hits are sure to
show up on Amsterdam's
screens after a short delay.
Films from other countries
occasionally make it to the
screen.
Almost all films are shown in
their original language, with
Dutch subtitles.

79

Classical Music & Opera

TICKET TIME

For theatre and concert performances at popular venues you generally need to book ahead. This can be done in person or by telephone to ticket reservation centres. From abroad tickets can be booked directly through the National Reservations Centre ☎ 31 70 3202500. For information and tickets, contact the Amsterdam Uit Buro's Ticketshop (✉ Leidseplein 26 ☎ 0900 0191 www.anb.nl Ⓘ Office open daily 10–6, Thu until 9; telephone answered 9–9 daily). Tickets for most performances can also be purchased from the VVV tourist offices and some hotels can book tickets for guests. The daily newspapers and listings magazine *Uitkrant* have programme details.

BEURS VAN BERLAGE

Home to the Netherlands Philharmonic Orchestra and Dutch Chamber Orchestra, this remarkable early modernist building that once housed the stock exchange now makes an impressive concert hall (➤ 56).
✉ Damrak 243   ☎ 6270466
🚊 Tram 4, 9, 16, 20, 24, 25

CONCERTGEBOUW

One of the world's finest concert halls, the magnificent neoclassical Concertgebouw has wonderful acoustics, making it a favourite with musicians worldwide. Since the Royal Concertgebouw Orchestra made its début in 1888, it has come under the baton of Richard Strauss, Mahler, Ravel, Schönberg and Haitink to name but a few. It continues to be one of the most respected ensembles in the world.
✉ Concertgebouwplein 2–6
☎ 6718345   🚊 Tram 3, 5, 12, 16, 20

IJSBREKER

A major international venue for contemporary classical music. There are performances of work by John Cage, Xanakis and other modern music pioneers, and around half the concerts are devoted to modern Dutch compositions.
✉ Weesperzijde 23
☎ 6939093   Ⓜ Weesperplein

MUZIEKTHEATER

Major operatic works and experimental opera from the Dutch National Opera and other leading international companies (➤ 57 and 79).
✉ Waterlooplein 22
☎ 6255455   Ⓜ Waterlooplein

NIEUWE KERK

Frequent lunchtime concerts and exceptional organ recitals by visiting organists, in an atmospheric setting (➤ 39).
✉ Dam   ☎ 6268168
🚊 Tram 1, 2, 4, 5, 9, 13, 14, 16, 17, 20, 24, 25

OUDE KERK

Chamber music concerts and organ recitals are held in this old church, where Holland's foremost composer, Jan Pieters' Sweelinck (1562–1621) was once organist. Pass by at 4PM on Saturdays, and you may hear a carillon concert (➤ 42).
✉ Oudekerksplein 23
☎ 6258284   Ⓜ Nieuwmarkt

RAI

This convention centre sometimes stages classical music and opera.
✉ Europaplein   ☎ 5491212
🚊 Tram 4

TROPENMUSEUM

Traditional music from developing countries is performed at the museum's Soeterijn Theater (➤ 50).
✉ Linnaeusstraat 2
☎ 5688215   🚊 Tram 6, 9, 10, 14, 20

WESTERGASFABRIEK

A popular venue for experimental opera.
✉ Haarlemmerweg 8–10
☎ 5810425   🚊 Tram 10; bus 18

Live Music

AKHNATON
Funky multicultural youth
centre with reggae, rap and
salsa dance nights. Be
prepared for close dancing
– this place gets full.
✉ Nieuwezijds Kolk 25
☎ 6243396 🚋 Tram 1, 2, 5,
13, 17, 20

ALTO JAZZ CAFÉ
One of Amsterdam's best
jazz and blues venues.
Live music nightly, pricey
drinks.
✉ Korte Leidsedwarsstraat 115
☎ 6263249 🚋 Tram 1, 2, 5,
6, 7, 10, 20

BAMBOO BAR
Tiny, dark and smoky, this
atmospheric bar plays
excellent live music
nightly – jazz, rhythm and
blues and salsa.
✉ Lange Leidsedwarsstraat 64
☎ 6243993 🚋 Tram 1, 2, 5,
6, 7, 10

BIMHUIS
The place for serious
followers of avant garde,
improvisational, and
experimental jazz,
attracting top international
players.
✉ Oudeschans 73
☎ 6231361 🚇 Nieuwmark

BOURBON STREET
Nightly blues and jazz.
✉ Leidsekruisstraat 6–8
☎ 6233440 🚋 Tram 6, 7, 10,
20

CANEÇAO
Brazilian bar with live
salsa nightly.
✉ Lange Leidsedwarsstraat 70
☎ 6261500 🚋 Tram 1, 2,
5, 6, 7, 10, 20

DE HEEREN VAN AEMSTEL
Prior to events such as the
North Sea Jazz Festival,
you can often see some of
the world's great jazz
performers here.
✉ Thorbeckeplein 5
☎ 6202173 🚋 Tram 4, 9,
14, 20

HOF VAN HOLLAND
Come here for an evening
of Dutch folk music and
traditional songs.
✉ Rembrandtplein 5
☎ 6234650 🚋 Tram 4, 9,
14, 20

MALOE MELO
This smoky yet convivial
Jordaan bar, Amsterdam's
'home of the blues', belts
out some fine rhythms.
✉ Lijnbannsgracht 163
☎ 4204592 🚋 Tram 3, 10

O'REILLY'S IRISH PUB
Choice whiskeys and
hearty Irish fare accom-
panied by jolly folk music.
✉ Paleisstraat 103–105
☎ 6249498 🚋 Tram 1, 2, 5

PARADISO
Amsterdam's best venue
for live acts – rock, reggae
and pop concerts, in a
beautiful old converted
church that was once the
haunt of 1960s hippies.
✉ Weteringschans 6–8
☎ 6264521 🚋 Tram 6, 7, 10

TWEE ZWAANTJES
Traditional Dutch enter-
tainment off the tourist
track in a tiny bar full of
accordion-playing, folk-
singing Jordaaners.
✉ Prinsengracht 114
☎ 6252729 🚋 Tram 13, 14,
17, 20

MELKWEG
Located in a wonderful old
dairy building (hence the
name *Melkweg* or 'Milky
Way') on a canal just off
Leidseplein, this off-beat
multimedia entertainment
complex opened in the 1960s
and remains a shrine to
alternative culture. Live bands
play in the old warehouse
most evenings, and there is
also a constantly changing
programme of unconventional
theatre, dance, art and film
events. (✉ Lijnbaansgracht
234 ☎ 6241777).

81

Brown Cafés & Other Bars

ANCIENT AND MODERN

Brown cafés, so-called because of their chocolate-coloured walls and dark wooden fittings, are reminiscent of the interiors in Dutch Old Master paintings. Here you can meet the locals in a setting that's *gezellig* (cosy). In stark contrast, there are a growing number of brasserie-like grand cafés, and chic, modern bars, with stylish, spacious interiors. Watch also for the tiny ancient *proeflokalen* tasting bars (originally distillers' private sampling rooms), with ageing barrels and gleaming brass taps, serving a host of gins and liqueurs.

BROWN CAFÉS

HANS EN GRIETJE

A small cosy bar beside one of Amsterdam's prettiest canals.
✚ E10 ✉ Spiegelgracht 27 ☎ 6241324 🚊 Tram 6, 7, 10

HOPPE

One of Amsterdam's most established, most popular brown cafés, with beer in one bar and gin from the barrel in another.
✚ F7 ✉ Spui 18–20 ☎ 4204420 🚊 Tram 1, 2, 5

DE KARPERSHOEK

A sawdust-strewn bar dating from 1629, and frequented by sailors.
✚ H3 ✉ Martelaarsgracht 2 ☎ 6247886 🚇 Centraal Station

HET MOLENPAD

An old-fashioned brown café. The canalside terrace catches the early evening sun.
✚ D8 ✉ Prinsengracht 653 ☎ 6259680 🚊 Tram 1, 2, 5

PAPENEILAND

Amsterdam's oldest bar resembles a scene from a Dutch Old Master painting, with its panelled walls, Makkum tiles, candles, benches and wood-burning stove.
✚ E2 ✉ Prinsengracht 2 ☎ 6241989 🚌 Bus 18, 22

DE PRINS

Very much a locals' bar, despite its proximity to the Anne Frankhuis, with a cosy pub atmosphere and seasonal menu.
✚ E3 ✉ Prinsengracht 124 ☎ 6249382 🚊 Tram 13, 14, 17, 20

VAN PUFFELEN

An intimate sawdust-strewn brown bar with a smart restaurant in the back. You can sit on a barge moored outside, on the Prinsengracht, in summer.
✚ D6 ✉ Prinsengracht 375–377 ☎ 6246270 🚊 Tram 13, 14, 17, 20

REIJNDERS

Brown cafés are typically on tranquil streets; Reijnders is on brash, neon-lit Leidseplein yet has retained much of its traditional style and look.
✚ D9 ✉ Leidseplein 6 ☎ 6234419 🚊 Tram 1, 2, 5, 6, 7, 10, 20

GRAND CAFÉS & STYLISH BARS

DE ENGELBEWAARDER

Jazz on Sunday from 4PM livens up a usually tranquil, arty hangout situated off the Red Light District.
✚ H6 ✉ Kloveniersburgwal 59 ☎ 6253772 🚇 Nieuwmarkt

DE JAREN

A spacious, ultramodern café, known for its trendy clientele and its sunny terraces overlooking the Amstel.
✚ G7 ✉ Nieuwe Doelenstraat 20–22 ☎ 6255771 🚊 Tram 4, 9, 14, 16, 20, 24, 25

DE KROON

A chic, colonial-style bar, with large potted plants, stuffed animals and wicker furniture.
✚ H8 ✉ Rembrandtplein 17 ☎ 6252011 🚊 Tram 4, 9, 14, 20

HET LAND VAN WALEM
One of Amsterdam's first modern bars.
➕ E8 ✉ Keizersgracht 449
☎ 6253544 🚋 Tram 1, 2, 5

LUXEMBOURG
Watch the world go by over canapés or colossal club sandwiches on the terrace of this elegant, high-ceilinged bar.
➕ F7 ✉ Spui 24
☎ 6206264 🚋 Tram 1, 2, 5

L'OPERA
Fashionable with the city's chic set.
➕ H8 ✉ Rembrandtplein 27–31 ☎ 6275232
🚋 Tram 4, 9, 14, 20

SCHILLER
An evocative art deco bar enhanced with live piano music. Sophisticated for Rembrandtplein.
➕ H8 ✉ Rembrandtplein 26
☎ 6249846 🚋 Tram 4, 9, 14, 20

PROEFLOKALEN (TASTING BARS)

CAFÉ HOOGHOUDT
Brown bar-cum-proeflokalen in an old warehouse lined with traditional stoneware jenever barrels. Tasty Dutch appetisers go with a big selection of liqueurs.
➕ H9 ✉ Reguliersgracht 11
☎ 4204041 🕐 4PM–1AM
🚋 Tram 4, 9, 14, 16, 20, 24, 25

DE DRIE FLESCHJES
Amsterdammers have been tasting gins at The Three Little Bottles since 1650.
➕ G5 ✉ Gravenstraat 18
☎ 6248443 🚋 Tram 1, 2, 4, 5, 9, 13, 14, 16, 17, 20, 24, 25

DE OOIEVAAR
A homely atmosphere pervades The Stork, one of Holland's smallest proeflokalen.
➕ G5 ✉ Sint Olofspoort 1
☎ 4208004 🚋 Centraal Station

SPECIALIST BARS

DE BEIAARD
A beer drinker's paradise – over 80 beers from around the world.
➕ F7 ✉ Spui 30
☎ 6225110 🚋 Tram 1, 2, 5

BROUWERIJ 'T IJ
Lethally strong beer brewed on the premises of the old De Gooier windmill (▶ 62).
➕ Q8 ✉ Funenkade 7
☎ 6228325 🕐 Wed–Sun 3PM–7:45PM 🚌 Bus 22, 28

BULLDOG PALACE
Flagship of the Bulldog chain of bars and smoking coffee shops – a plush, loud bar, brashly decked out in stars and stripes. Downstairs is a 'smoking coffeeshop'. (▶ 71).
➕ D9 ✉ Leidseplein 13–17
☎ 6271908 🚋 Tram 1, 2, 5, 6, 7, 10, 20

CYBER C@FÉ
The first of several internet cafés in Amsterdam.
➕ G3 ✉ Nieuwendijk 19
☎ 6235146 🚋 Centraal Station

CAFÉ APRIL
Popular, easy-going gay bar that attracts a mixed crowd of mostly male locals and tourists.
➕ F8 ✉ Reguliersdwarsstraat 37 ☎ 6259572 🚋 Tram 1, 2, 5

BAR TALK
Most of the 1,402 bars and cafés in Amsterdam are open from around 10AM in the early hours and many serve meals. Proeflokalen open from around 4PM until 8PM, and some serve snacks, such as nuts, cheese, meatballs and sausage. Beer is the most popular alcoholic drink. It is always served with a head, and often with a jenever chaser called a kopstoot (a blow to the head). If you want only a small beer, ask for a colatje or Kleintjepils. Dutch for cheers is Proost!

'DUTCH COURAGE'
Dutch gin (jenever), made from molasses and flavoured with juniper berries, comes in a variety of ages: jong (young), oud (old) and zeer oud (the oldest and the mellowest), and in colour ranging from clear to brownish. Other flavours may be added; try bessenjenever (blackcurrant), or bitterkoekjes likeur (macaroon). Jenever is drunk straight or as a beer chaser, not with a mixer.

Nightclubs

GAY AMSTERDAM

Clubbing is at the heart of Amsterdam's gay scene. The best-known venue is iT, a glitzy disco with throbbing techno. Gay bars and clubs abound in nearby Reguliersdwarsstraat and Halvemaansteeg. To find out exactly what's on and where it's happening, call the Gay and Lesbian Switchboard (☎ 6236565) or read the bilingual (Dutch–English) magazines *Gay News* and *Gay & Night*.

NIGHT AT THE TABLES

Try all the usual games, plus Sic Bo (a Chinese dice game) at Holland Casino, one of Europe's largest. There is a small entrance fee and you must be over 18 and present your passport, but there is no strict dress code.
✚ G6 ✉ Max Euweplein 62
☎ 5211111 🚊 Tram 1, 2, 5, 6, 7, 10, 20

BOSTON CLUB

Attracts a 30s–40s crowd looking for a quieter dancing experience.
✚ H4 ✉ Renaissance Hotel, Kattengat 1 ☎ 5512030
🚉 Centraal Station

DANSEN BIJ JANSEN

Student disco, playing the latest chart toppers.
✚ H5 ✉ Handboogstraat 11
☎ 6201779 🕙 11PM–4AM
🚊 Tram 1, 2, 5,

ESCAPE

Amsterdam's largest disco can hold 2,000 dancers. Dazzling light show, superb sound system.
✚ H5 ✉ Rembrandtplein 11
☎ 6223542 🕙 10PM– 4AM
(Fri, Sat until 5AM) 🚊 Tram 4, 9, 14, 20

iT

The wildest disco in town, with outrageously dressed clientele and fierce house music. Saturday night is exclusively gay.
✚ H5 ✉ Amstelstraat 24
☎ 6250111 🕙 Thu, 11PM–4AM; Fri, Sat 11PM–5AM
🚊 Tram 4, 9, 14, 20

MARGARITAS

An intimate Caribbean club combining cool cocktails with hot dancing – to the latest salsa and *merengu*e beats.
✚ H5 ✉ Reguliersdwarsstraat 108 ☎ 6257277
🕙 Fri, Sat 11:30PM–5AM; Sun 11:30PM–4AM 🚊 Tram 1, 2, 5, 16, 20, 24, 25

MAZZO

A young image-conscious crowd prop up the bar of this small but chic disco in the Jordaan, while guest DJs and live bands play

the latest sounds.
✚ G5 ✉ Rozengracht 114
☎ 6267500 🕙 11PM–4AM
(Fri, Sat 5AM) 🚊 Tram 13, 14, 17, 20

MINISTRY

A café-cum-nightclub with all kinds of disco music.
✚ H5 ✉ Reguliersdwarsstraat 12 ☎ 6233981 🕙 Thu–Mon 10PM–5AM 🚊 Tram 1, 2, 5, 16, 20, 24, 25

ODEON

A converted canal house with house music on the first floor, 1960s–'80s classic disco upstairs and jazz in the basement.
✚ H5 ✉ Singel 460
☎ 6249711 🕙 10PM–4AM
(Fri, Sat 5AM) 🚊 Tram 1, 2, 5

SEYMOUR LIKELY 2

Jazz dance, soul, disco, reggae and hip-hop in trendy 'post-nuclear fallout' surroundings.
✚ H5 ✉ Nieuwezijds Voorburgwal 161 ☎ 4205062
🕙 Mon–Thu 9PM–3AM; Fri, Sat 9PM–4AM 🚊 Tram 1, 2, 5, 13, 17

TRANCE BUDDHA

The city's biggest trance club complete with Indian decoration.
✚ H5 ✉ Oudezijds Voorburgwal 216 ☎ 4228233
🕙 Mon–Thu 11PM–4AM; Fri, Sat 11PM–5AM 🚊 Tram 1, 2, 5, 13, 17, 20

SOUL KITCHEN

Leading 'non-house' club for soul, funk and weekly retro theme nights.
✚ H5 ✉ Amstelstraat 32
☎ 6202333 🕙 Wed–Mon 11PM–5AM 🚊 Tram 4, 9, 14, 20

Sport

FISHING
Obtain a permit from the Dutch Fishing Federation to fish in the Amsterdamse Bos (► 60).
🔶 H6 ✉ Nicolaas Witsenstraat 10 ☎ 6264988 🚃 Tram 6, 7, 10

FITNESS
JANSEN AEROBIC FITNESSCENTRUM
Fitness centre with gyms, sauna, solarium and daily aerobics classes.
🔶 H5 ✉ Rokin 109 ☎ 6269366 🚃 Tram 4, 9, 14, 16, 20, 24, 25

GOLF
GOLFBAAN WATERLAND
Modern 18-hole course just north of the city centre.
🔶 L1 ✉ Buikslotermeerdijk 141 ☎ 6361010

HORSE RIDING
HOLLANDSCHE MANEGE
Amsterdam's most central riding school dating from 1882.
🔶 F6 ✉ Vondelstraat 140 ☎ 6180942 🚃 Tram 1, 6

JOGGING
There are marked trails for joggers through the Vondelpark and Amsterdamse Bos. The Amsterdam Marathon is in May, and the Grachtenloop canal race in June when up to 5,000 run either 5, 10, or 20km along the banks of Prinsengracht and Vijzelgracht.

ICE SKATING
The canals often freeze in winter, turning the city into a big ice rink. Skates can be bought at most sports equipment stores.

JAAP EDENBAAN
A large indoor ice rink, open October to March.
🔶 L7 ✉ Radioweg 64 ☎ 6949652 🚃 Tram 9

SWIMMING
The seaside is only 30 minutes away by train, with miles of clean, sandy beaches. Zandvoort is closest; Bergen and Noordwijk are also popular.

FLEVOPARKBAD
The best outdoor pool in the city, open from mid-May until late-September.
🔶 M6 ✉ Zeeburgerdijk 630 ☎ 6925030 🚃 Tram 14

DE MIRANDABAD
Subtropical swimming pool complex, with indoor and outdoor pools, beach and wave machines.
🔶 H8 ✉ De Mirandalaan 9 ☎ 6428080 🚌 Bus 60, 158

BUNGY JUMPING
BUNGY JUMP HOLLAND
Jump from a crane 74m above the water, a half a kilometre east of Centraal Station. If you can open yours eyes, the views are unforgettable.
🔶 K4 ✉ Oostelijke Handelskade 1 ☎ 4196005 🚌 Bus 22

GO-KARTING
KAARTBAAN
Great fun for children large and small.
🔶 B3 ✉ Theemsweg 10 ☎ 6111642 🚉 Sloterdijk

SPECTATOR SPORTS
Football is Holland's number one spectator sport and the number one team is Ajax Amsterdam. Watch them play at their magnificent new stadium, the Amsterdam ArenA, ArenaBoulevard, Amsterdam Zuidoost (☎ 3111333). Other popular events include international field hockey at Wagenaar Stadium (✉ Nieuwe Kalfjeslaan ☎ 6401141) and equestrian show-jumping at RAI (✉ Europaplein ☎ 5491212) every November. Look out for a Dutch hybrid of volleyball and netball called *korfball*, and *carambole* – billiards on a table without pockets.

Luxury Hotels

PRICES

Expect to pay over 180 euros/
f400 a night for a double room
in a luxury hotel.

HOTEL TIPS

Two-fifths of Amsterdam's
30,000 hotel beds are in 4-
and 5-star properties, making
problems for people looking
for mid-range and budget
accommodation. At peak
times, such as during the
spring tulip season and
summer, empty rooms in
lower-cost hotels are about as
rare as black tulips. Book
ahead for these times.
Special offers may be available
at other times. Many hotels
lower their rates in winter,
when the city is quieter and
truer to itself than in the mad
whirl of summer.
Watch out for hidden pitfalls,
such as Golden Age canal
houses with four floors, steep
and narrow stairways and no
lift; and tranquil-looking
mansions with a late-night
café's pavement terrace next
door.
The VVV operates a hotel
reservation centre from
Mon–Fri 9–5 ☎ (31) 77 700
0088 (from outside the
Netherlands).

AMERICAN

Resplendent art-nouveau
Amsterdam classic on the
Leidseplein. 188 rooms.
✚ D9 ✉ Leidsekade 97,
Grachtengordel ☎ 5563000
🚊 Tram 1, 2, 5, 6, 7, 10, 20

AMSTEL INTER-CONTINENTAL

Holland's most luxurious
and expensive hotel, on
the Amstel river, is a little
way from the centre, but
provides a motor yacht
and luxury limousines to
make sightseeing easier.
79 rooms.
✚ K11 ✉ Prof Tulpplein 1,
Grachtengordel ☎ 6226060
🚊 Weesperlein 🚊 Tram 6, 7,
10, 20

BILDERBERG GARDEN

In a pleasant leafy suburb,
a short tram ride from the
city centre. 98 rooms.
✚ Off map
✉ Dijsselhofplantsoen 7, Oud
Zuid ☎ 6642121 🚊 Tram 16

BLAKES AMSTERDAM

A stunning 17th-century
conversion designed by
Anouska Hempel with
individually-furnished
accommodation based on
Dutch and Indonesian
themes. 26 rooms.
✚ D7 ✉ Keizersgracht 384,
Grachtengordel ☎ 5302010
🚊 Tram 1, 2, 5

DE L'EUROPE

Prestigious, combining
turn-of-the-century
architecture with the most
modern amenities, in a
waterfront setting. 100
rooms.
✚ G7 ✉ Nieuwe Doelenstraat
2–8, Centrum ☎ 5311777
🚊 Tram 4, 6, 9, 14, 16, 20,
24, 25

GOLDEN TULIP BARBIZON PALACE

Modern luxury deftly
concealed within a row of
17th-century mansions.
274 rooms.
✚ H4 ✉ Prins Hendrikkade
59–72, Centrum ☎ 6201207
🚊 Centraal Station

GRAND HOTEL KRASNAPOLSKY

Built in the 1880s, the
'Kras' has belle-époque
grace in its public spaces
and modern facilities in its
rooms. 469 rooms.
✚ G5 ✉ Dam 9, Centrum
☎ 5549111 🚊 Tram 1, 2, 4,
5, 9, 13, 14, 16, 17, 20, 24, 25

GRAND SOFITEL DEMEURE

Once a 16th-century royal
inn, then the City Hall,
now a luxury hotel. 182
rooms.
✚ H4 ✉ Oudezijds
Voorburgwal 197, Centrum
☎ 5553111 🚊 Nieuwmarkt

HILTON

Modern efficiency, on a
leafy boulevard to the
south. The honeymoon
suite was the scene of John
Lennon and Yoko Ono's
weeklong 1969 love-in for
world peace. 271 rooms.
✚ Off map ✉ Apollolaan 138,
Oud Zuid ☎ 7106000
🚊 Tram 16

PULITZER

Twenty-four 17th-century
houses, once the homes of
wealthy merchants, have
been converted into this
luxurious canalside hotel.
226 rooms.
✚ D5 ✉ Prinsengracht
315–331, Grachtengordel
☎ 5235235 🚊 Tram 13, 14,
17, 20

Mid-Range Hotels

AMBASSADE
Amsterdam's smartest B&B, in a series of gabled canal houses. 59 rooms.
➕ E7 ✉ Herengracht 335–353, Grachtengordel ☎ 5550222 🚊 Tram 1, 2, 5

AMSTERDAM
Fully modernised behind its 18th-century façade, on one of the city's busiest tourist streets. 80 rooms.
➕ G5 ✉ Damrak 93–94, Centrum ☎ 5550666 🚊 Tram 4, 9, 14, 16, 20, 24, 25

AMSTERDAM HOUSE
Quietly situated small hotel beside the Amstel. Most rooms have a view of the river. 16 rooms.
➕ H7 ✉ 's-Gravelandseveer 3, Centrum ☎ 6246607 🚊 Tram 4, 9, 14, 16, 20, 24, 25

CANAL HOUSE
Antique furnishings and a pretty garden make this small, family-run hotel on the Keizersgracht a gem. 26 rooms.
➕ E4 ✉ Keizersgracht 148, Grachtengordel ☎ 6225182 🚊 Tram 13, 14, 17, 20

ESTHERÉA
A well-considered blend of wood-panelled canalside character with efficient service and modern facilities. 70 rooms.
➕ F6 ✉ Singel 303–309, Grachtengordel ☎ 6245146 🚊 Tram 1, 2, 5

GOLDEN TULIP DOELEN
Amsterdam's oldest hotel, the place where Rembrandt painted *The Night Watch*, with small rooms, but well-equipped. 85 rooms.
➕ G7 ✉ Nieuwe Doelenstraat 24, Centrum ☎ 5540600 🚊 Tram 4, 9, 14, 16, 20, 24, 25

JAN LUYKEN
A well-run, elegant town-house hotel in a quiet back street near Vondelpark and the Museumplein. 62 rooms.
➕ C11 ✉ Jan Luijkenstraat 58, Oud Zuid ☎ 5730717 🚊 Tram 2, 3, 5, 12

MAAS
A charming, family-run, waterfront hotel round the corner from Leidseplein, near museums, shops and nightlife. Some rooms have waterbeds. 28 rooms.
➕ D9 ✉ Leidsekade 91, Grachtengordel ☎ 6233868 🚊 Tram 1, 2, 5, 6, 7, 10, 20

PRINSENGRACHT
A quiet hotel, with a garden, on one of the city's most beautiful canals. 34 rooms.
➕ G10 ✉ Prinsengracht 1015, Grachtengordel ☎ 6237779 🚊 Tram 4, 16, 24

REMBRANDT RESIDENCE
On Amsterdam's most celebrated canal. 111 rooms.
➕ E6 ✉ Herengracht 255, Grachtengordel ☎ 6236638 🚊 Tram 13, 14, 17, 20

SEVEN BRIDGES
Small and exquisite, with a view of seven bridges, lots of antiques and owners who treat their guests as though they were family friends. 11 rooms.
➕ H10 ✉ Reguliersgracht 31, Grachtengordel ☎ 6231329 🚊 Tram 16, 24, 25

PRICES
Expect to pay from 90 euros/ f200 to 180 euros/f400 a night for a double room in a mid-range hotel.

BED AND BREAKFAST, APARTMENTS AND BOATS
If you want to rent an apartment in Amsterdam, contact Amsterdam House (✉ Amstel 176a ☎ 6262577; e-mail: www.amsterdamhouse.com); you can take your pick of luxury apartments in converted canal houses, or even a houseboat. Bed and Breakfast Holland (✉ Theophile de Bockstraat 3, ☎ 6157527) will set you up in a private house.

MODERN SCHOOL
The Tulip Inn, with its striking modern Amsterdam School-style architecture has particularly good facilities for visitors with disabilities.
➕ F6 ✉ Spuisstraat 288–292, Centrum ☎ 4204545 🚊 Tram 1, 2, 5

Budget Accommodation

PRICES

Expect to pay up to 90 euros/ f200 a night for a double room in a budget hotel. Hostels and campsites are considerably cheaper.

CAMPING

There are several campsites in and around Amsterdam. The best-equipped one is a long way out, in the Amsterdamse Bos (✉ Kleine Noorddijk 1, ☎ 6416868). Vliegenbos is just a ten-minute bus ride from the station, close to the River IJ (✉ Meeuwenlaan 138, ☎ 6368855). Contact the VVV for full details.

ACACIA

An inexpensive, cheerful, family-run hotel in the Jordaan, with studio rentals and a houseboat that sleeps four. 14 rooms.
✚ D3 ✉ Lindengracht 251, Jordaan ☎ 6221460 🚊 Tram 3

AGORA

A small, comfortable, 18th-century canal house furnished with antiques and filled with flowers. 16 rooms.
✚ F7 ✉ Singel 462, Grachtengordel ☎ 6272200 🚊 Tram 4, 9, 14, 16, 20, 24, 25

AMSTEL BOTEL

One of Amsterdam's few floating hotels, with magnificent views over the old docks. 175 rooms.
✚ J4 ✉ Oosterdokskade 2–4, Oost and Oosterdok ☎ 6264247 🚇 Centraal Station

ARENA

A large hostel and information centre for youthful travellers. It has a café and restaurant (with garden terrace), and puts on dance nights, concerts, exhibitions and other events. 121 rooms.
✚ M10 ✉ 's-Gravesandestraat 51, Oost and Oosterdok ☎ 6947444 🚊 Tram 3, 6, 10

DE FILOSOOF

Each room in this unique hotel is named after the great philosophers and decorated accordingly. 25 rooms.
✚ Off map ✉ Anna van den Vondelstraat 6, Oud West ☎ 6633201 🚊 Tram 1, 6

NJHC CITY HOSTEL VONDELPARK

A wide range of modern options, from dormitories to family rooms. 475 rooms.
✚ C10 ✉ Zandpad 5, Vondelpark, Oud Zuid ☎ 5898996 🚊 Tram 1, 2, 5, 6, 20

NOVA

A clean, simple, central hotel, with friendly young staff. 59 rooms.
✚ F6 ✉ Nieuwezijds Voorburgwal 276, Centrum ☎ 6230066 🚊 Tram 1, 2, 5

OWL

Family-owned hotel with bright, comfortable rooms and a garden, in a quiet street near Vondelpark. 34 rooms.
✚ C10 ✉ Roemer Visscherstraat 1, Oud Zuid ☎ 6189484 🚊 Tram 2, 3, 5, 12

PRINSENHOF

Quaint, comfortable and clean. One of the city's best budget options. 11 rooms.
✚ H10 ✉ Prinsengracht 810, Grachtengordel ☎ 6231772 🚊 Tram 4

SINT-NICOLAAS

Rambling former factory and comfortable, if sparse, facilities. 24 rooms.
✚ G4 ✉ Spuistraat 1a, Centrum ☎ 6261384 🚊 Tram 1, 2, 5, 13, 17, 20

VAN OSTADE BICYCLE HOTEL

Small hotel that rents bikes and gives advice on how to discover hidden Amsterdam by bicycle. 16 rooms.
✚ Off G11 ✉ Van Ostadestraat 123, De Pijp ☎ 6793452 🚊 Tram 3, 4

AMSTERDAM
travel facts

ESSENTIAL FACTS

Electricity
- 220 volts; round two-pin sockets.

Etiquette
- Shake hands on introduction. Once you know people better, you might exchange three pecks on alternate cheeks instead.
- Remember to say *hallo* and *dag* (goodbye) when shopping.
- Dress is generally informal, even for the opera, ballet and theatres.
- Although service charges are included in bills, tipping is customary. Leave a small tip or round up the bill.

Money matters
- Banks may offer a better exchange rate than hotels or independent bureaux de change. GWK (Grebswusselkantor) offer 24-hour money-changing services at Schiphol Airport and Centraal Station.

National holidays
- 1 January; Good Friday, Easter Sunday and Monday; 30 April; Ascension Day; Pentecost and Pentecost Monday; 25 and 26 December.
- 4 and 5 May – Remembrance Day (*Herdenkingsdag*) and Liberation Day (*Bevrijdingsdag*) – are World War II Commemoration Days but not public holidays.

Opening hours
- Banks: Mon–Fri 9 until 4 or 5. Some stay open Thu until 7.
- Shops: Tue–Sat 9 or 10 until 6, Mon 1 to 6. Some open Thu until 9 and Sun noon until 5. Some close early Sat, at 4 or 5.
- State-run museums and galleries: most open Tue–Sat 10 to 5, Sun and national holidays 1 to 5. Many close on Mon.

Places of worship
- Roman Catholic: Parish of the Blessed Trinity, Heilige Familie-kerk ☒ Zouiersweg 180 ☎ 4652711
- English Reformed Church: ☒ Begijnhof 48 ☎ 6249665
- Jewish: Jewish and Liberal Community Amsterdam: ☒ Jacob Soetendorpstraat 8 ☎ 6423562
- Muslim: THAIBA Islamic Cultural Centre: ☒ Kraaiennest 125 ☎ 6982526

Student travellers
- For discounts at some museums, galleries, theatres, restaurants and hotels, students under 26 can obtain an International Young Person's Passport (CJP – Cultureel Jongeren Passpoort), cost 9 euros/f20, from: AUB ☒ Leidseplein 26 ☎ 0900 0191; and NBBS ☒ Rokin 66 ☎ 6240989

Toilets
- There are few public toilets. Use the facilities in hotels, museums and cafés. There is often a small charge.

Tourist offices (VVV)
- The five main Vereniging Voor Vreemdelingenverkeer (VVV) offices all have multilingual staff, city maps and brochures. They will also make hotel, excursion, theatre and concert bookings for a small fee. They are:
Centraal Station VVV
➕ J3 ☒ Centraal Station, Platform 2)
Stationsplein VVV
➕ J4 ☒ Stationsplein 10
Leidseplein VVV
➕ D9 ☒ Leidseplein 1
Stadionplein VVV
➕ Off map ☒ Argonautenstraat 9 and

Holland Tourism International at
Schiphol Airport (🕂 Off map).
• For enquiries ☎ 0900 4004040;
www.visitamsterdam.nl; info@amsterdamtourist.nl

PUBLIC TRANSPORT

Buying and using tickets
• If you intend to use public transport frequently, buy a ticket of 15
or 45 strips (*strippenkaart*), available at GVB and Dutch Railways
ticket counters and the VVV. For
each ride, a strip must be stamped
for each zone you want to pass
through, plus one for the ride: for
example, from Centraal Station to
Leidseplein is two zones, so you
need to stamp two strips of your
strippenkaart, plus one more. Zones
are shown on maps at tram, bus
and Metro stops.
• On buses: tell the driver the
number of zones you want and
your ticket will be stamped.
• On the Metro or light railway:
before boarding, fold back the
appropriate number of strips and
punch your ticket in the yellow
ticket machines on the station.
• On trams: either ask the driver to
stamp your ticket or do it yourself in a yellow punch-machine.
Some trams have a conductor at
the back who sells and stamps
tickets.
• For a single trip, purchase a 'one-
hour' ticket, from the driver of the
bus or tram, or from a machine at
the Metro entrance. Buy day and
other tickets, 2-, 3-, 8-, 15- and 45-
strip cards from Metro and train
station ticket counters, VVV
offices, newsagents and bus/tram
drivers.
• All tickets are valid for one hour
after the time stamped on them,
and include transfers.

• Don't travel without a valid ticket:
you could be fined 27 euros/f60 on
the spot.
• For further information and maps,
contact GVB 🕂 J4 ✉ Stationsplein
☎ 0900/9292

Getting around by bicycle
• The best way to see Amsterdam is
by bicycle. To hire one costs from
4.50 euros/f10 a day, 17 euros/f38
a week.
Damstraat Rent-a-Bike 🕂 G6
✉ Pieter Jacobszoondwarsstraat 11 ☎ 6255029
BikeCity 🕂 D5 ✉ Bloemgracht 68–70
☎ 6263721 🕔 Mon–Sat 9–6

MEDIA & COMMUNICATIONS

Mail
• Purchase stamps (*postzegels*) at
post offices, tobacconists and
souvenir shops.
• Post boxes are bright red and
clearly marked 'ptt post'.

Newspapers and magazines
• The main Dutch newspapers are
De Telegraaf (right wing), *De
Volkskrant* (left wing) and *NRC
Handelsblad*.
• The main Amsterdam news-
papers (sold nationwide) are *Het
Parool* and *Nieuws van de Dag*.
• Listings magazines: *What's on in
Amsterdam* and *Uitkrant*.
• *The Times*, the *Independent* and
the *Guardian* are widely
available.

Post Offices
• Most post offices open weekdays
8:30 or 9 until 5.
• Main Post Office: 🕂 F5
✉ Hoofdpostkantoor PTT, Singel 250–256
☎ 5563311 🕔 Mon–Fri 9–6 (Thu 9–8);
Sat 10–1:30
• Postal Information: ☎ 0900/0417

Telephones

- Most public telephones take phonecards available from telephone centres, post offices, railway stations and newsagents.
- Phone calls within Europe cost about 0.45 euros/f1 per minute.
- Information: ☎ 0900/8008
- International information: ☎ 0900/0418
- Numbers starting 0900 are premium rate calls.
- Local and international operator: ☎ 0800/0410
- To phone abroad, dial 00 then the country code (UK 44, US and Canada 1, Australia 61, New Zealand 64), then the number.
- Most hotels have International Direct Dialling, but it is expensive.
- The code for Amsterdam is 020. To phone from outside Holland drop the first 0.

EMERGENCIES

Emergency phone numbers

- Police: ☎ 112
- Ambulance: ☎ 112
- Fire Service: ☎ 112
- Tourist Medical Service: ☎ 6245793 (day), 5923355 (24hr)
- Automobile Emergency (ANWB): ☎ 0900 5031040
- Lost credit cards: American Express ☎ 5048666, Diners Club ☎ 5573407, Master/Eurocard ☎ 030/2835555, Visa ☎ 6600611
- Sexual Advice ☎ 6166222
- Crisis Helpline ☎ 6757575

Embassies and consulates

- American Consulate: ✚ Off C11 ✉ Museumplein 19 ☎ 57553309
- British Consulate: ✚ Off map ✉ Koningslaan 44 ☎ 6764343
- Canadian Embassy: ✉ Sophianlaan 7, The Hague ☎ 070/3111600
- Australian Embassy: ✉ Carnegielaan 4a, The Hague ☎ 070/3108200
- New Zealand Embassy: ✉ Carnegielaan 10, The Hague ☎ 070/3469324
- Irish Embassy: ✉ Dr Kayperstraat 9, The Hague ☎ 070/3630993
- South African Embassy: ✉ Wassenaarseweg 40, The Hague ☎ 070/3924501

Lost property

- For insurance purposes, report lost or stolen property to the police as soon as possible.
- Main lost property offices: Centraal Station ✚ J3 ✉ Stationsplein 15 ☎ 5578544 ③ 7AM–11PM daily; Police Lost Property ✚ Off map ✉ Steffersonstraat 18 ☎ 5593005 ③ Mon–Fri noon–3:30
- For property lost on public transport, GVB ✚ J4 ✉ Prins Hendrikkade 108–14 ☎ 4605858 ③ Mon–Fri 9–4

Medicines

- For non-prescription drugs, bandages and so on, go to a *drogist*.
- For prescription medicines, go to an *apotheek*, most open Mon–Fri 8:30–5:30.
- Details of pharmacies open outside normal hours are in the daily newspaper *Het Parool* and all pharmacy windows.
- The Central Medical Service (☎ 020/5923434) can refer you to a duty GP or dentist.
- Hospital outpatient clinics are open 24 hours a day. The most central is Onze Lieve Vrouwe Gasthuis ✚ M11 ✉ 1e Oosterparkstraat 279 ☎ 5999111 🚊 Trams 3, 10, 17

Precautions

- Pickpockets are common in busy shopping streets and markets, and in the Red Light District. Take sensible precautions and remain

on your guard at all times.
- At night, avoid poorly lit areas and keep to busy streets. Amsterdam is not dangerous, but muggings do occur.
- There are no particular risks to women travelling alone. For information contact the Vrouwenhuis (Women's House) ✉ Nieuwe Herengracht 95 ☎ 6252066

LANGUAGE

Basics

yes	ja
no	nee
please	alstublieft
thank you	dank u
hello	hallo
good morning	goedemorgen
good afternoon	goedemiddag
good evening	goedenavond
good night	welterusten
goodbye	dag
breakfast	het ontbijt

Useful words

good/bad	goed/slecht
big/small	groot/klein
hot/cold	warm/koud
new/old	nieuw/oud
open/closed	open/gesloten
push/pull	duwen/trekken
entrance/exit	ingang/uitgang
men's/women's bathroom	heren/damen wc
free/occupied	vrij/bezet
far/near	ver/dichtbij
left/right	links/rechts
straight ahead	rechtdoor

Restaurant

breakfast	het ontbijt
lunch	de lunch
dinner	het diner
menu	de kaart
winelist	de wijnkaart
main course	het hoofdgerecht
dessert	het nagerecht
the bill, please	mag ik afrekenen

Numbers

1	een	15	vijftien
2	twee	16	zestien
3	drie	17	zeventien
4	vier	18	achtien
5	vijf	19	negentien
6	zes	20	twintig
7	zeven	21	eenentwintig
8	acht	22	tweeëntwintig
9	negen	30	dertig
10	tien	40	veertig
11	elf	50	vijftig
12	twaalf	100	honderd
13	dertien	1,000	duizend
14	veertien		

Days and times

Sunday	Zondag
Monday	Maandag
Tuesday	Dinsdag
Wednesday	Woensdag
Thursday	Donderdag
Friday	Vrijdag
Saturday	Zaterdag
today	vandaag
yesterday	gisteren
tomorrow	morgen

Useful phrases

Do you speak English? Spreekt u engels?

Do you have a vacant room? Zijn er nog kamers vrij?

with bath/shower met bad/douche

I don't understand Ik versta u niet

Where is/are ..? Waar is/zijn?

How far is it to ..? Hoe ver is het naar?

How much does this cost? Hoeveel kost dit? …

What time do you open? Hoe laat gaat u open?

What time do you close? Hoe laat gaat u dicht?

Can you help me? Kunt u mij helpen?

93

Index